FINANCIAL ACCOUNTING AND STATEMENT ANALYSIS: A MANAGER'S GUIDE

FINANCIAL ACCOUNTING AND STATEMENT ANALYSIS: A MANAGER'S GUIDE

Almand R. Coleman
*Distinguished Lecturer in Accounting,
Washington and Lee University
Charles C. Abbott Professor of
Business Administration, Emeritus*

E. Richard Brownlee, II
*Associate Professor of
Business Administration*

C. Ray Smith
*Professor of
Business Administration*

*The Colgate Darden Graduate School of
Business Administration
University of Virginia*

Reston Publishing Company, Inc.
A Prentice-Hall Company
Reston, Virginia

TO OUR FAMILIES

© 1982 by Reston Publishing Company, Inc.
A Prentice-Hall Company
Reston, Virginia 22090

All rights reserved. No part of this publication
may be reproduced, stored in a retrieval system,
or transmitted, in any form or by any means,
electronic, mechanical, photocopying, recording,
or otherwise, without prior written permission of
the publisher.

ISBN 0-8359-1987-0

PRINTED IN THE UNITED STATES OF AMERICA

10   9   8   7   6   5   4   3   2

Designed and typeset by Publications Development Co.
of Crockett, Texas, Developmental Editor: Nancy Marcus
Land, Production Editor: Bessie Graham

Preface

This book was written primarily for nonfinancial managers and executives desiring to gain a better understanding of financial accounting and financial statement analysis without getting bogged down in accounting "mechanics" or accounting terminology. It should also be useful to both undergraduate and graduate students looking for a nontechnical reference text to enhance their understanding and interpretation of financial statements.

Our approach throughout the book is intended more for the user of financial accounting information than for the preparer, as we focus on developing an understanding of figure relationships and accounting concepts instead of on the mastery of accounting techniques. Consequently, our presentation differs in a number of respects from more traditional financial accounting-related books. Our presentation of accounting fundamentals is limited to those we feel are essential to understanding the accounting process and the uses and limitations of financial statements prepared in accordance with generally accepted accounting principles. We generally avoid the use of "debit" and "credit" and speak, instead, in terms of account increases and decreases. We also treat revenues and expenses as direct adjustments to retained earnings.

The role of financial accounting and reporting increased substantially during the decades of the 1960s and 1970s as a result of such phenomena as prolonged double-digit inflation and the drastic decline in the financial stability of several major U.S. cities and corporations. These occurrences also caused individuals, businesses, and government agencies to begin placing greater importance on cash-flow analysis. We believe the cash-flow consequences of business activities will continue to have a high management priority during the 1980s and so have placed considerable emphasis throughout the book on cash-flow analysis and the relationship between income and cash flow. In the final chapter entitled "Accounting for Changing Prices," we discuss inflation from both an accounting and a management perspective.

As we have observed that many of the difficulties people experience in understanding financial accounting originate from a general unfamiliarity with accounting terminology, we have tried to minimize these language-related problems in two ways. First, we have avoided using "accounting terminology" whenever we felt that less technical language would serve equally as well; and second, we have prepared a rather extensive Glossary that appears in the Appendix. Through these and other somewhat unconventional means, we have attempted to produce a book that will serve the needs of a variety of present and future managers.

Acknowledgments

The authors are indebted to our colleagues on The Darden School Faculty—Brandt Allen, Bill Harper, Cathy Kahn, and Bill Rotch—for their suggestions in improving the eariler drafts of the material in this book.

Wilson Goh and Nancy Tower, student research assistants, were particularly helpful in the final preparation of the manuscript. We also benefited from the many contributions made by our students in the past several years.

The two former Deans of The Darden School, Charles Abbott and Stewart Sheppard, and the current Dean, Robert Haigh, have been most generous in their support and encouragement. Dean Edward Atwood at Washington and Lee University, where Mr. Coleman is currently Distinguished Lecturer in Accounting, has also provided strong encouragement. Our friend for many years, Robert Dame, has been the driving force in motivating us to prepare the book for publication. His associate, Nancy Marcus Land, has been most helpful in editing and producing the final product.

Our secretaries have typed from drafts that even we had difficulty reading. We are particularly grateful to Karen Dickinson, Zelma Watson, and Dorothea Govoruhk.

And, finally, we gratefully acknowledge the sincere interest and faithful support of our families.

Almand R. Coleman
E. Richard Brownlee, II
C. Ray Smith

Contents

Preface		*v*
Chapter 1.	**Accounting: A Contemporary Perspective** Nature and Purpose of Accounting • Types of Accounting Reports • A Corporate Emphasis • Generally Accepted Accounting Principles • Fundamental Accounting Concepts • Summary	1
Chapter 2.	**Traditional Financial Statements** Assets, Liabilities, and Owners' Equity • Balance Sheet • Income Statement • Statement of Retained Earnings • Summary	15
Chapter 3.	**The Accounting Process** Business Events • Accounts and the Double-Entry System of Accounting • Analysis of Business Transactions • Corner Drugstore's Transactions for One Year • Trial Balance • The Report Form of Balance Sheet • Combined Statement of Income and Retained Earnings • Comparative Financial Statements • Remarks About the Approach • Summary	31
Chapter 4.	**Statement of Changes in Financial Position** The Statement's Form and Content • Preparation of the Statement • Reconstruction of Accounts • The Statement Illustrated • Limitations of External Financial Statements • Summary	51

Chapter 5.	**Cash, Cash Equivalent, and Cash Flow**	65

Changes in Assets: A Trading Company • Changes in Assets: A Manufacturing Company • Managing Changes in Assets • Current Assets, the Operating Cycle, and the Current Ratio • The Nature of Cash and Cash Equivalent • Cash Management and Compensating Balances • Cash in Bank: Checks and Deposits • Cash and Cash Equivalent on the Balance Sheet • Statement of Cash Receipts and Disbursements • Cash Flow Statement • Cash Flow Statements Derived from Company Annual Reports • Learning from the Cash Flow Statement • Fraud and Internal Control • Summary

Chapter 6.	**Annual Reports to Stockholders**	91

Statement of Income and Retained Earnings • Statement of Financial Position • Statement of Changes in Financial Position • Auditor's Opinion • Some Controversies in Contemporary Accounting • Summary

Chapter 7.	**Analysis of Financial Statements**	115

The Company and Its Environment • Preparation of Income Statement for Analysis • Preparation of Statement of Financial Position for Analysis • Conversion of Statement of Changes in Financial Position to a Cash Flow Statement • Ratio Analysis of Financial Statements • Receivable Collection Period, Inventory Turnover, and Current Ratio • Debt Ratios • Stockholders' Equity and Earnings Ratios • Summary

Chapter 8.	**Accounting for Changing Prices**	137

Traditional Financial Statements • Financial Reporting and Changing Prices • Financial Statement Presentation • Limitations and Usefulness of Financial Information Adjusted for Changing Prices • Summary • Appendix A

Glossary	161
Index	175

1

Accounting: A Contemporary Perspective

This introductory chapter discusses the role of accounting in the contemporary United States business environment. The nature and purpose of accounting are presented, with emphasis placed on financial accounting principles and practices as they pertain to corporations.

The dynamic nature of America's business and economic environment was never more evident than during the 1970s. The combination of double-digit inflation, rising unemployment, drastic increases in the price of oil, energy shortages, and high interest rates produced an environment that was considerably different at the end of the decade than it had been at the beginning. During the latter part of the 1970s, many businesses reported record earnings, yet claimed that these earnings were more fictitious than real. The blame for this alleged misrepresentation of corporate profitability was placed largely on the accounting profession for not responding in a timely fashion to the need for some type of inflation accounting. Serious questions were raised by investors, creditors, and other external users of corporate financial information as to the usefulness of financial data reported in accordance with the traditional accounting concepts of "historical cost" and "constant dollars." These users argued that prolonged inflation resulted in a business and economic environment that could no longer be meaningfully represented by financial statements based on existing accounting concepts and principles.

Because reported corporate financial information plays such an important role in determining how and where business and economic resources are allocated, financial representation of economic reality during the inflationary period of the 1970s was a major concern, not just of the accounting profession and its critics, but of businesses, not-for-profit organizations, government, and society in general. What people wanted was a relevant, unbiased, and understandable financial reporting system capable of providing an accurate accounting of business and economic activity during a period of rapidly rising prices. Accountants were called upon to develop such a reporting system but were unable to agree on how it should be done.

The widespread interest in and confusion over the extent to which reported corporate profits were "real" eventually resulted in congressional concern that perhaps the establishment of generally accepted accounting principles, upon which financial reporting is based, is too important a task to be left to the accountants. After considerable investigation and deliberation, Congress decided to allow the establishment of accounting principles to remain in the private sector but recommended more active participation in the entire standard-setting process by those outside the accounting profession. The end result of all the attention directed toward accountants, accounting principles, and corporate financial reporting was both a better informed public regarding the role of accountants in society and a more dynamic and responsive accounting profession.

NATURE AND PURPOSE OF ACCOUNTING

The extensive publicity of the 1970s helped to dispel at least some of the misunderstandings people had about accounting and accountants. Before commencing with a discussion of the nature and purpose of contemporary accounting, it is important to mention a few of the common misconceptions about accounting. Contrary to popular belief, accounting is *not*

- Unchanging and unimaginative.
- Difficult or impossible to understand.
- Concerned only with taxes.
- Mathematically complex.
- Among the most effective known cures for insomnia.
- Best suited to men who are short, thin, slightly bald, wear green eyeshades, and live alone.

Although this list of common accounting misconceptions is far from complete, it does illustrate the type of thinking that has served to inhibit an understanding of accounting and the profession. Let's avoid any such mistake by setting aside all preconceived notions as we begin to look at what accounting really is.

Accounting may be defined as "... the process of identifying, measuring, and communicating economic information to permit informed judgments and decisions by users of the information."[1] Not too many years ago, accountants were generally thought of primarily as clerks rather than as interpreters of financial data. As businesses and their environments increased in complexity, however, the nature and scope of accounting changed considerably. Accounting in the 1980s is an interesting, challenging, and rewarding profession that requires considerable analytical ability.

In a broad sense, accounting may be thought of as a service activity that provides financial information about an economic entity that is useful in making rational investment, credit, and similar decisions. Relevance and reliability are the two primary qualities that make accounting information useful for decision making.[2] Accounting serves as the financial measurement and communication system for both profit and nonprofit organizations. Because of its vital communicative aspects, accounting is often referred to as the "language of business."

---

[1] *A Statement of Basic Accounting Theory* (Evanston, Illinois: American Accounting Association, 1966), p.1.

[2] A discussion of other qualities of accounting information can be found in Statement of Financial Accounting Concepts No. 2, *Qualitative Characteristics of Accounting Information* (Stamford, Connecticut: Financial Accounting Standards Board, 1980).

FINANCIAL AND MANAGEMENT ACCOUNTING

Accounting may be subdivided into two classifications based on the intended purpose of the data presented. *Financial accounting* provides users "external" to an organization with quantitative information regarding its economic resources, obligations, and financial performance. External users include investors, creditors, various government agencies, and the general public. *Management accounting* provides essentially the same information to "internal" users such as management and the Board of Directors.

Even though the information needs of internal and external users are similar, there are several important reasons for distinguishing between financial and management accounting. First, management needs financial data more frequently and in greater detail than do external users. Second, the form and content of the accounting reports for management are of unlimited flexibility. By contrast, reports prepared for external users often must conform to standards defined by the accounting profession or various regulatory agencies. Third, external users' decisions are principally financial, whereas those of management are both financial and operational.

TYPES OF ACCOUNTING REPORTS

Three general types of accounting reports are prepared by business organizations. These are external financial statements, internal financial reports for management, and income tax reports.

External financial statements are those contained in annual reports to stockholders and filings with various governmental organizations. Also included are the financial statements submitted to banks and other financial institutions.

The external financial statements of one organization may also be used by another organization to appraise the issuer's desirability as a customer or as a possible investment opportunity. For organizations in similar businesses, external reports provide information useful in evaluating the competition. The distinguishing characteristic of external financial statements is that they are prepared in accordance with certain established standards called "generally accepted accounting principles."

In order for management to make ongoing decisions regarding past, present, and future business operations, *internal financial reports* are usually prepared more frequently and in considerably more detail than is customary for external financial reporting. Although internal reporting includes the same types of information contained in the financial statements prepared for external users, management needs additional data about such things as cost allocation, cost control, and performance measurement and evaluation. Because internal reports do not have to conform to generally accepted accounting principles, their form and content depend on factors such as the decisions to be made, the availability of data, and the cost associated with preparing the reports.

Income tax reports are prepared periodically by profit-oriented organizations. Specific tax reporting formats have been developed by federal, state, and local tax authorities to be used by businesses in determining their taxes. Although the income tax laws generally require that taxable income be calculated in accordance with generally accepted accounting principles, a number of major differences do exist between the contents of a company's external financial statements and its tax return.

Notwithstanding our emphasis on financial accounting, the perspective taken herein is principally that of how management uses financial statements prepared in accordance with existing generally accepted accounting principles. In addition, the management perspective will necessitate consideration of the usefulness of published financial information to investors, creditors, and other external users. Accounting is a means to an end and is so presented throughout this book.

A CORPORATE EMPHASIS

Because of the dominance of the corporate form of organization in terms of the aggregate dollar volume of U.S. business activity, the emphasis throughout this text will be on accounting for profit-oriented corporations. There are, however, relatively few differences between corporate accounting and accounting for proprietorships and partnerships.

Probably the most commonly used definition of a corporation is the one given in 1819 by Chief Justice Marshall in the Dartmouth College case. He stated: "A corporation is an artificial being, invisible, intangible, and existing only in contemplation of the law." It is created when a corporate charter is issued by one of the states subsequent to the submission of required legal documents and the payment of the incorporation fee to the state's Corporation Commission. Once established, a corporation may issue stock certificates to its owners, take title to property, enter into contractual agreements, incur debts, sue and be sued, and conduct such business as stated in its charter. Corporations whose stock is widely held are known as public corporations, whereas those whose stock is held by relatively few owners are called private or close corporations.

One of the first responsibilities of the stockholders is to elect a Board of Directors who become responsible for the overall management of the corporation. The directors, in turn, elect the corporate officers whose duties involve the day-to-day management of the corporation. The officers usually include a president, vice-president, secretary, and treasurer. They report periodically to the Board of Directors, whose management role is largely advisory and supervisory in nature. During the 1970s, many large corporations increased the number of "outside" directors in an attempt to give their Boards greater independence from the corporate officers. Outside directors are those who are associated with the corporation only in their role as directors. By 1980, the average number of directors of large U.S. corporations was fifteen, of which ten were outside directors.

Corporations hold an annual meeting of stockholders subsequent to the end of each fiscal year. A *fiscal year* is the twelve-month period a corporation has selected as its accounting year, and it may or may not be the calendar year. The annual meeting is held for such purposes as reviewing the year's financial performance, discussing business, economic, and political issues of importance to the corporation, selecting the accounting firm to perform the following year's independent audit of the corporation's financial records, electing directors whenever vacancies on the Board exist, and transacting any other business that requires ratification by the stockholders.

The stock of many public corporations is bought and sold daily on the various stock exchanges. Even though such changes in corporate ownership represent private transactions among investors, corporations must keep an up-to-date record of their stockholders. When shares of stock are sold, the seller assigns the stock certificate representing the number of shares sold to the buyer and sends the certificate to the corporation. The corporation cancels the certificate received and issues a new one in the name of the purchaser. As long as the stock is purchased from an existing stockholder and not from the corporation, the only effect on the corporation is a change in its *stockholders of record*. Many corporations engage the services of a transfer agent and registrar to cancel old stock certificates, issue new ones, and maintain a current record of stockholder names and addresses and the number of shares owned by each stockholder. Transfer agents and registrars are usually banks and trust companies.

Public corporations also issue annual reports to stockholders and other interested parties. These reports generally include letters to stockholders from both the chairman of the Board and the president, a description of the company, audited financial statements, the report of the independent accountants, and management's discussion of past performance and future goals and objectives. The accountant's report states whether, in the opinion of the independent accounting firm, the financial statements presented in the annual report were prepared in accordance with *generally accepted accounting principles* applied on a basis consistent with the previous year.

GENERALLY ACCEPTED ACCOUNTING PRINCIPLES

Financial accounting is based on a set of standards that have evolved over time through the efforts of numerous individuals and organizations. These standards, known as generally accepted accounting principles, provide the basis upon which corporate financial reporting is based. Although the term "principles" creates the impression of immutability, this is not the case. Changing business and economic conditions require a continual monitoring of generally accepted accounting principles (GAAP) to ensure their relevance to contemporary environments. The name also suggests the existence of a complete and comprehensive list of such principles. This, however, is not the case. Let's briefly look at why.

Generally accepted accounting principles can be thought of as the ground rules that govern the preparation of corporate external financial statements. In the United States, these principles have developed in the same way as English Common Law; they are manmade, accumulate case-by-case, and are subject to continual revision. Accounting principles can become generally accepted only after they have obtained substantial authoritative support from the business community and related organizations.

Historically, three organizations have been particularly influential in establishing accounting principles: the American Institute of Certified Public Accountants (AICPA), the American Accounting Association (AAA), and the Securities and Exchange Commission (SEC). Two significant events in the early 1930s laid the foundation for the development of GAAP. In 1934, a special committee was formed by the AICPA and the New York Stock Exchange (NYSE) to develop an approach and a philosophy toward establishing accounting principles. The committee's concluding report contained the following passage:

> The more practical alternative would be to leave every corporation free to choose its own methods of accounting within the very broad limits to which reference has been made, but require disclosure of the methods employed and consistency in their application from year to year....
>
> Within quite wide limits, it is relatively unimportant to the investor which precise rules or conventions are adopted by a corporation in reporting its earnings if he knows what method is being followed and is assured that it is followed consistently from year to year....[3]

In essence, the committee rejected the idea of compelling all companies to use identical accounting principles regardless of circumstances and accepted, instead, the idea of establishing broad standards upon which individual organizations could base their accounting principles and procedures. In short, the concept of uniformity in accounting principles was discarded in favor of reasonable flexibility coupled with full disclosure and consistency. Once adopted by a company, however, the selected principles had to be followed consistently from year to year. Thirty years after this committee published its recommendations, a member of the accounting profession underscored the significance of the committee's approach as follows:

> In spite of the fact that the committee was the first to use the term "accepted principles of accounting" and the first to attempt a formal statement of accounting principles, its most important contribution was more basic. The fundamental framework of accounting

[3] *Audits of Corporate Accounts* (New York: American Institute of Certified Public Accountants, 1934), p. 9.

which the committee established has guided the development of accounting for thirty years. The recommendations were not fully implemented, but the basic concept which permitted each corporation to choose those methods and procedures which were most appropriate for its own financial statements within the basic framework of "accepted accounting principles" became the focal point of the development of principles in the United States.[4]

The second major event was the establishment of the Securities and Exchange Commission (SEC). Through the Securities Act of 1933 and the Securities Exchange Act of 1934, Congress created the SEC and charged it with the responsibility of protecting the public from false and misleading information. Publicly-owned corporations were required to disclose financial and other data in a manner that fairly represented the underlying economic events. Congress gave the SEC broad authority to establish accounting principles and reporting standards. Rather than exert its authority directly, the SEC chose instead to allow these principles and standards to be set by the private sector. This decision has remained unchanged. A close working relationship continues to exist between the SEC and the AICPA, the organization in the private sector that for many years was recognized by the SEC as having the responsibility for establishing accounting principles. As will be discussed shortly, this responsibility now rests primarily with the Financial Accounting Standards Board (FASB).

During the more than forty years since the SEC decided to allow the private sector to develop accounting principles, several different groups of accounting and financial experts have participated in the process. In 1938, the AICPA organized its *Committee on Accounting Procedure* specifically for this purpose. During its twenty-year existence, the Committee issued 51 Accounting Research Bulletins. Its approach was primarily practical: the Committee developed "principles" as the need arose in actual problem situations. During this same period, the American Accounting Association (AAA) was also actively involved in establishing accounting principles. The approach taken by the AAA was more theoretical; the AAA attempted to establish a broad set of interrelated, consistent, and comprehensive standards. The AAA believed that "real world" problems could then be solved by accounting procedures developed in conformity with

---

[4] Reed K. Storey, *The Search for Accounting Principles* (New York: American Institute of Certified Public Accountants, 1964), p. 12.

these standards. Of the two organizations, the AICPA had the greater impact on the practice of accounting.

By the mid-1950s, the need for more research and for a "theoretical accounting framework" became evident. In 1959, the AICPA formed the Accounting Principles Board (APB) to supersede the Committee on Accounting Procedure. The AICPA intended that the Accounting Principles Board would emphasize accounting research and would articulate a theoretical framework. The Accounting Principles Board never quite achieved its goals, however, primarily because the accounting issues it faced were too urgent, complex, and time consuming to permit much theoretical work. During its fourteen-year existence, the APB issued 31 "Opinions" and 4 "Statements." The former were pronouncements that the Board considered authoritative. The latter were merely informative reports without official status.

In 1973, the Accounting Principles Board was superseded by the Financial Accounting Standards Board (FASB). Unlike the Committee on Accounting Procedure and the APB, the FASB is not part of the AICPA. It is an independent organization comprised of seven members who report to a nonprofit corporation known as the Financial Accounting Foundation (FAF). Financial support for the FASB is received from six sponsoring organizations: the American Institute of Certified Public Accountants, the National Association of Accountants, the American Accounting Association, the Financial Executives Institute, the Financial Analysts Federation, and the Securities Industry Association. By the end of 1980, the FASB had issued over 40 "Statements of Financial Accounting Standards." Subsequent to the formation of the FASB, the term *standards* has largely replaced the term *principles* in the accounting profession. We use these two terms interchangeably in this text.

FUNDAMENTAL ACCOUNTING CONCEPTS

The development of accounting principles in the United States has been greatly enhanced by the identification and acceptance of certain broad fundamental accounting concepts. In this section, those concepts that have had the greatest effect on financial accounting and reporting practices are briefly discussed.

Business Entity. A business entity is an organization that sells products and/or services at a profit. When external financial reports are presented, the business entity should be clearly identified. If a single owner conducts several separate proprietorships—for example, a laundry, a dairy, and a drugstore—each of these entities should be clearly identified and reported upon separately. When the business entity is a corporation, it should be made clear that the financial statements are those of the business which is separate and distinct from its owners. When one corporation owns more than fifty percent of the capital stock of other corporations, the external financial statements of the entire group are usually presented on a "consolidated" basis. When this occurs, the business entity is identified as the consolidated group of corporations.

Going Concern. External financial reports are prepared based upon the assumption that the business entity will continue to operate indefinitely and will not be liquidated in the foreseeable future. No attempt is made to disclose the financial effects of sudden liquidation.

Accounting Period. For purposes of measuring financial performance and financial position, the life of a business is divided into discrete time periods. The most common accounting period is twelve months in length and is known as a fiscal year.

Objectivity. Business transactions are recorded only when they can be supported by reasonable and verifiable evidence.

Historical Dollar Accounting. Transactions of a business entity are recorded in its accounting records in terms of dollars at the time each transaction occurs. Because these accounting records contain dollars recorded at different times, summarization adds together dollars of different vintages without recognizing their differences in purchasing power. The double-digit inflation of the 1970s caused the usefulness of this concept to be seriously questioned by external users of corporate financial statements.

Realization. This concept refers to the time when a business should recognize sales revenue. Ordinarily, revenue is realized at the time title to goods passes to the buyer or the service is performed. Realization usually does not depend on the timing of the cash receipts.

Matching. This concept pertains to the timing of the recognition of associated revenues and expenses. Generally, expenses should be recognized during the same accounting period as are the revenues to which the expenses relate.

Use of Estimates and Exercise of Judgment. Financial statements are not as precise as they usually appear. Financial reports are prepared for designated periods and points of time, but because time is a continuum, business transactions do not always fit neatly into designated accounting periods. This results in the need for estimates and judgments.

Consistency Between Periods. So that external users may compare financial reports for the same entity over several years, it is essential that they be prepared on a consistent basis from year to year. If changes occur in reporting methods or accounting principles, the reports should disclose the reason for and the effects of such changes.

Diversity in Accounting. Users of external financial reports should expect to find some diversity in accounting and reporting among business entities. Accounting authorities disagree as to the degree of diversity that should be tolerated. Most authorities believe, however, that accountants should try to narrow the range of divergence in "generally accepted accounting principles" to the end that there may be more comparability of reporting among companies.

Conservatism. When several acceptable alternatives exist for the preparation of external financial reports, the choice should be made in favor of "conservative" reporting. Accordingly, the report must provide for all known losses and liabilities regardless of whether they are definitely quantifiable, but must not anticipate income until it is definitely realized. In short, provide for all losses but do not anticipate income.

Materiality. External financial reports should disclose all essential information, yet be uncluttered with the trivial. Materiality of information is determined by whether its disclosure would alter the judgment or conduct of the intended users.

SUMMARY

As the language of business, accounting is expected to provide both internal and external users with relevant and reliable financial information about an organization that is useful in making rational investment, credit, and similar decisions. Financial accounting pertains specifically to providing external users with data about an organization's resources, obligations, and financial performance. Financial accounting is governed by generally accepted accounting principles that must be adhered to in the preparation of external financial statements. These principles are based on certain broad fundamental accounting concepts. Neither the concepts nor the principles are immutable, however, and both are continually evaluated to ensure their relevance to a changing environment. As became particularly evident during the 1970s, accounting plays a vital role in the allocation and use of business and economic resources. As the United States enters a new decade, the accounting profession will be expected to make whatever changes are necessary in external financial reporting to provide users with relevant data upon which to base their decisions.

2

Traditional Financial Statements

In this chapter, the balance sheet, income statement, and statement of retained earnings are illustrated and discussed. Also presented is the importance of the fundamental accounting equation to the preparation and understanding of these three financial statements.

Traditionally, businesses have periodically prepared three basic financial statements as a means of assessing the financial consequences of their activities. These are the *balance sheet* (also known as the *statement of financial position*), the *income statement*, and the *statement of retained earnings*. The income statement and the statement of retained earnings are often combined into a single statement. In 1971, the Accounting Principles Board added a fourth basic financial statement, the *statement of changes in financial position*.

For external purposes, corporations normally publish their financial statements annually. Annual financial reporting is often supplemented by the issuance of quarterly financial statements. For internal purposes, financial statements may be prepared on a monthly, weekly, or any other basis. Regardless of the frequency of their preparation, internal financial statements generally include substantially greater detail than those prepared for external use.

ASSETS, LIABILITIES, AND OWNERS' EQUITY

To describe the contents and purposes of all the basic financial statements, we will trace the business activities of a small, closely-held corporation, Corner Drugstore, Inc., from the date of incorporation through the first several years of its existence. We will begin by looking at its financial status immediately following the approval of its charter by the State Corporation Commission and the issuance of capital stock to the owners on April 3, 1978.

Specific requirements for incorporation are established by state law and are reasonably uniform among the states. Incorporation may be accomplished by one or more individuals, and there frequently exists a minimum legal requirement as to the amount of the owners' initial investment. In exchange for their investment, the owners receive shares of capital stock issued by the newly formed corporation. These shares provide written evidence of ownership in the corporation and are distributed to the owners in proportion to their share of the total amount invested in the corporation.

In the case of Corner Drugstore, two incorporators each invested $5,000 cash in exchange for an equal number of shares of capital stock. Immediately thereafter, the new corporation owned by the two stockholders consisted of only one financial resource, cash, in the amount of $10,000. This initial financial position would have been reflected on the drugstore's balance sheet prepared as of the date of incorporation.

The purpose of a balance sheet is to present an enterprise's resources, obligations, and the amount of the owners' investment, all as of a specified point in time. The resources are known as *assets*, the obligations as *liabilities*, and the owners' investment as *owners' equity*. To elaborate, assets are all items of value, tangible or intangible, that a business owns. Liabilities are debts or obligations. Owners' equity refers to the total investment of the owners at the balance sheet date. For corporations, owners' equity is referred to as stockholders' equity. Subsequent to incorporation, Corner Drugstore had one asset, $10,000 in cash, no liabilities, and owners' equity of $10,000.

The relationship between assets (A), liabilities (L), and owners' equity (OE) is the foundation of accounting. This fundamental relationship is expressed as follows:

$$A = L + OE$$

Traditional Financial Statements

At any time, a company's assets always equal the sum of its liabilities and owners' equity. Keeping in mind that assets are things of value owned by a business, that liabilities are debts or obligations, and that owners' equity represents the owners' total investment, we can see that the equation makes good common sense. It simply states that the assets of a business must always equal the sources of those assets. These sources are the *owners* and the *creditors*, the latter being individuals or organizations providing assets in exchange for the corporation's promise of payment or repayment at a later date.

As its name suggests, the equality of an enterprise's assets and its liabilities and owners' equity is always reflected on the *balance sheet*. In recent years, the balance sheet has increasingly been referred to as the *statement of financial position*.

BALANCE SHEET ILLUSTRATED

Let us suppose that at the end of its first year of existence Corner Drugstore had the following assets, liabilities, and owners' equity:

Assets:	
Cash on hand and in bank	$ 2,500
Due from customers	4,200
Merchandise inventory	12,700
Store equipment (cost $10,000)	9,000
Liabilities:	
Owed to suppliers	$ 3,800
Owed to employees	700
Owed to utilities	200
Federal and state taxes owed	2,300
Owed to bank	7,500
Owners' equity:	
Capital stock issued	$10,000
Retained earnings	3,900

Before elaborating upon any of these items, let's see how they would appear on Corner Drugstore's balance sheet. Although a balance sheet may be prepared in several different forms, the "account form" is illustrated here as it is the one most commonly used.

The first thing to notice about the balance sheet is its heading. A proper heading for any type of financial statement should answer these questions:

1. WHO? That is, the name of the business whose financial data are being reported.
2. WHAT? That is, the name of the statement itself—balance sheet, income statement, etc.
3. WHEN? That is, the *point in time* or the *period of time* to which the statement relates.

In Illustration 2-1, the heading answers these three questions as follows:

1. WHO? Corner Drugstore, Inc.
2. WHAT? Balance Sheet
3. WHEN? March 31, 1979

Notice two things about the date of this balance sheet. First, like all balance sheets, this one applies only to a specific point in time. The

---

Illustration 2-1

Corner Drugstore, Inc.
Balance Sheet
March 31, 1979

Assets		Liabilities	
Cash	$ 2,500	Accounts payable	$ 3,800
Accounts receivable	4,200	Wages payable	700
Merchandise inventory	12,700	Utilities payable	200
Store equipment		Taxes payable	2,300
(cost $10,000)	9,000	Bank loan payable	7,500
		Total liabilities	14,500
		Owners' Equity	
		Capital stock $10,000	
		Retained earnings 3,900	13,900
		Total liabilities &	
Total assets	$28,400	owners' equity	$28,400

balance sheet can be thought of as a snapshot of the business entity's financial position. Second, Corner Drugstore has chosen to end its fiscal year on March 31. As mentioned in Chapter 1, a fiscal year is the accounting year over which a business reports its activities and at the end of which it prepares financial statements for external use. A fiscal year is usually selected so that it ends at a time when business activity is comparatively slow and the amount of merchandise on hand is relatively low. Businesses may choose any fiscal year period that they wish, and it is possible to change fiscal years. Companies frequently select the calendar year as their fiscal year because it ends immediately following a period of heavy sales.

Assets Explained

The assets of Corner Drugstore are representative of those of most retail establishments. Cash is the first asset listed on most balance sheets. The amount shown in Illustration 2-1 represents the store's total cash balance on March 31, 1979, whether it was physically located at the store or held in deposit by a bank. The term "accounts receivable" (or trade receivable) represents the amount owed to the drugstore by customers who purchased merchandise but as of March 31 had not yet paid for those purchases. From the drugstore's perspective, such customer purchases represented "credit sales" or "sales on account." Instead of receiving cash at the time of sale, Corner Drugstore received customers' promises to pay cash at some future time, often within 30 days.

The merchandise inventory figure of $12,700 represents the total *cost* of all salable merchandise that the drugstore owned at fiscal year-end, such as toiletries, drugs, toys, and small appliances. It is not uncommon for retail stores to display merchandise that they do not own. Such merchandise is "on consignment" to the retailer. For example, magazines are often placed in drugstores on consignment. If the Corner Drugstore had any merchandise on consignment in its store on March 31, 1979, this merchandise would not have been included in the balance sheet figure of $12,700 because such merchandise was not owned by the drugstore.

The $9,000 amount for store equipment is a little more difficult to explain. During the fiscal year, Corner Drugstore purchased display counters, shelves, cash registers, and various other types of store equipment. The total cost of all such purchases was $10,000, and all were paid for in cash. At the time these purchases occurred, the drugstore simply traded one asset for another; specifically, cash was given in exchange for store equipment. Total assets remained unchanged, and liabilities and owners' equity were unaffected. The $9,000 figure shown for store equipment in Illustration 2-1 represents the *unallocated cost* of the equipment at fiscal year-end. The $1,000 difference represents the *allocated cost*.

"Allocated to what?" is a question that will be answered more fully later in this chapter. For the moment, let's view cost allocation as follows: The store equipment was estimated by the owners of Corner Drugstore to have a useful life of 10 years. At the end of that period, the owners expected that the equipment would have no value to the drugstore. Because assets represent items having value to a business, at the end of the 10-year period the store equipment could no longer appear as an asset on the balance sheet. The allocation process permits the $10,000 initial cost of the store equipment to be reduced to $0 over the 10-year period. In this case, $1,000 of the cost would be "allocated" or "written off" the balance sheet each year for 10 years. Recalling the accounting equation, $A = L + OE$, we realize that if the allocation process reduces assets, then either liabilities or owners' equity must also be reduced. In fact, owners' equity is reduced, the reasons for which will be explained further on in this chapter.

Liabilities and Equity

Liabilities are represented on the balance sheet according to the type of creditor. A *creditor* is an individual or organization providing a business with an asset or assets in exchange for its promise to pay cash at some later date. Accounts Payable represents the amount owed by a business for merchandise that it purchased; Wages Payable are wages earned by employees but not yet paid; Utilities Payable represents the amount owed for utilities at the balance sheet date; Taxes Payable reflects the amount owed to federal and state governments for taxes imposed on the profits earned by the drugstore during the fiscal year. The Bank Loan Payable was incurred because Corner Drugstore did not have enough cash to acquire all of the assets that it needed to do business. Shortly after incorporating, the drugstore borrowed $9,000 from a local bank. The loan was to be repaid in equal installments on March 31 each year for 6 years. The first installment was paid to the bank in 1979. Although interest rates had begun to rise, the previous relationships that the two owners had with the bank allowed Corner Drugstore to negotiate a 5 percent interest rate. Interest on the unpaid balance was also due annually on March 31.

The owners' equity in Corner Drugstore at the end of its first fiscal year consisted of the owners' original investment of $10,000 (the amount shown for capital stock on the balance sheet) and $3,900 retained earnings. This $3,900 figure means that as a result of all of the business transacted at the drugstore during its first year of existence, the excess of assets over liabilities (a relationship known as *net assets*) increased by $3,900. The drugstore's net assets on the date of incorporation had been $10,000 ($10,000 in assets less $0 in liabilities). As the owners did not invest anything beyond their $10,000 original amount (capital stock at fiscal year-end was still $10,000), the increase in net assets of $3,900 had to be attributed to profitable operations. Understanding the concepts of "profits" and "operations" requires a discussion of the second basic financial statement—the income statement.

INCOME STATEMENT ILLUSTRATED

The income statement that Corner Drugstore prepared at the end of its first fiscal year is shown in Illustration 2-2. As we did with the balance sheet, let's begin by looking at the questions answered by the statement's heading.

1. WHO?   Corner Drugstore, Inc.
2. WHAT?   Income Statement
3. WHEN?   Fiscal Year Ended March 31, 1979

Notice that, unlike the balance sheet, the income statement covers a *period of time*. It presents the results of the operations of a business entity over a specified period of time, usually a fiscal year for statements prepared for external use.

Revenues

The purpose of the income statement is to show the change in owners' equity during an accounting period arising from the sale of

Illustration 2-2

Corner Drugstore, Inc.
Income Statement
For the Fiscal Year Ended March 31, 1979

Gross sales		$75,800
Less: Sales returns		1,300
Net sales		74,500
Deduct: Cost of merchandise sold		44,700
Gross margin on sales		29,800
Less Operating expenses:		
Employees' wages	$15,300	
Rent	3,600	
Utilities	650	
Allocated cost of store equipment	1,000	
Other	500	
Total operating expenses		21,050
Income from operations		8,750
Less: Interest on bank loan		450
Income before income taxes		8,300
Less: Federal and state income taxes		2,900
Net income		$ 5,400

products and/or services to customers, less the cost of the products and/or services sold, and less any other expenses incurred during the period. The income statement consists of two major components—revenues and expenses. *Revenue* is the increase in an organization's net assets (assets less liabilities) resulting from the sale of a product or service. *Expense* is the decrease in an organization's net assets that occurs in connection with the revenue generation process; that is, the sale of products and/or services.

At Corner Drugstore, revenue arose from the sale of merchandise. In generating this revenue, the store incurred various expenses. The difference between the total amount of revenues and the total amount of expenses is known as *net earnings, net profit*, or *net income*. These three terms are used interchangeably to refer to the net change in owners' equity arising from day-to-day business operations. The specific revenues and expenses for Corner Drugstore that resulted from its first year of operations are shown in Illustration 2-2. These are typical for any type of merchandising business.

The total sales price of all merchandise sold by Corner Drugstore is reflected in the *gross sales* amount of $75,800. Merchandise is considered to be sold at the time that the title to the merchandise (ownership of the merchandise) passes from the seller to the buyer. In the case of the drugstore, a sale occurred when a customer received merchandise and, in return, provided the drugstore with cash or a promise to pay cash at a future date. Pay particular attention to what has just been said. A sale occurs when ownership of merchandise transfers from seller to buyer, *not* when the seller receives cash from the buyer. In the case of cash sales, the transfer of ownership to the buyer and the receipt of cash by the seller occur simultaneously. Such is not the case, however, for sales that are made to customers "on credit." For credit sales, the seller records a sale at the time ownership transfers, but because no cash is received from the buyer at that time, the seller records an account receivable. We know from Illustration 2-1 that Corner Drugstore made credit sales because the March 31 balance sheet contains $4,200 in accounts receivable. A fundamentally important concept is to be learned from this discussion: revenue is recognized when earned, regardless of whether cash has been exchanged. Additionally, the receipt of cash by a business does not necessarily mean that revenue has simultaneously been earned.

Like most merchandising organizations, Corner Drugstore had some of its sales returned by customers during the year. The amount of such returns is shown in the income statement as sales returns. In the case of Corner Drugstore, sales returns amounted to $1,300. Gross sales less sales returns is known as *net sales*. Net sales represent the actual sales for the period.

Expenses

The *cost of goods sold* figure of $44,700 represents the actual cost to the drugstore of the merchandise that was sold at a total sales price of $74,500. The $29,800 difference between net sales and cost of goods sold is referred to as *gross margin* or *gross profit*. The relationship between net sales and gross margin is important, and businesses watch it quite carefully to make sure it does not get "out of line" because of changes in either selling prices or the cost of merchandise sold.

The *operating expenses* shown in the income statement represent items that decreased net assets but were necessary in order for the drugstore to maintain its day-to-day operations. As might be expected, the largest operating expense was compensating employees for their services. We can also see that the drugstore incurred rent expense for use of the building in which it was located, and utilities expense for light, heat, power, etc. As no "building" asset appeared on the balance sheet in Illustration 2-1, we could have concluded at the time we discussed the drugstore's assets that it didn't own a building and, therefore, must have been renting the facility in which it was located.

The $1,000 expense called *allocated cost of the store equipment* reflects the gradual allocation to expense of the $10,000 cost of the store equipment purchased during the fiscal year. The "process of cost allocation" was described earlier in the chapter when we discussed the $9,000 figure for store equipment listed as an asset on the March 31, 1979 balance sheet. At that time, we stated that the effect of such a cost allocation was to reduce the dollar amount shown for store equipment from its original cost of $10,000 to the unallocated cost of $9,000.

We also said that in addition to reducing the asset amount by $1,000, the allocation also reduced owners' equity by a like amount. The allocation diminished owners' equity because it represented an operating expense (commonly known as *depreciation*), was listed as an expense on the income statement, and reduced the amount of the net income. We can conclude from this example that all expenses reduce owners' equity and that all revenues increase owners' equity. We shall see shortly why these relationships exist.

The "other expenses" of $500 represent the total amount of the miscellaneous expenses incurred during the year. These would include expenses for postage, advertising, and various supplies (payroll taxes have been ignored). If we subtract the total operating expenses from the amount of the gross margin, we get $8,750 *income from operations*. This figure represents the income that was earned by the drugstore during the year from its day-to-day operations. Two additional expenses of considerable importance must then be deducted to determine the amount of the increase in owners' equity during the year that was attributable to the overall business activities. These two expenses are *interest* and *income taxes*.

We know from our discussion of Illustration 2-1 that Corner Drugstore borrowed $9,000 from a local bank shortly after incorporating. We also know that on March 31, 1979, Corner Drugstore paid the bank one-sixth of the amount borrowed or *principal* of the loan plus an amount for interest. Interest is the fee that a bank charges a borrower for the use of the money borrowed, the amount of which is determined by three factors: the amount borrowed, the length of the loan, and the rate of interest. In this case, the bank charged Corner Drugstore a 5 percent interest rate.

The amount of interest to be charged is calculated in accordance with the following formula:

$$\text{Interest} = \text{Principal} \times \text{Annual Interest Rate} \times \text{Time (expressed as a fraction of a year)}$$

Thus,

$$I = P \times R \times T$$

Applying this formula to the bank loan granted to Corner Drugstore, we get:

$$I = (\$9{,}000) \times (.05) \times (1); \text{ so } I = \$450$$

By subtracting the interest expense from the income from operations, we get "income before income taxes." The $2,900 amount for federal and state income taxes represents that portion of the *pretax income* of $8,300 to which the federal and state governments have a legal claim. The remaining $5,400 represents *net income*. The drugstore's owners' equity was increased by this amount during the year as the result of the store's business operations.

It is important to understand that at no time during our discussion of the expenses shown in the income statement did we make any reference to cash. Expenses are shown in the income statement during the period in which they are incurred; that is, during the period in which they cause the net assets of a business to be reduced. Whether or not actual cash disbursements were made during the period in connection with the expense item does not affect their recognition as expenses. In those cases where cash disbursements were made for an expense, net assets decreased because the asset, cash, decreased. In those cases where cash disbursements were *not* made for an expense, net assets decreased because a liability increased or some asset other than cash decreased. We can see these liabilities on the balance sheet in Illustration 2-1. As of March 31, 1979, Corner Drugstore owed $700 in wages to employees, $200 for utilities, and $2,300 in federal and state taxes. These are liabilities because the drugstore incurred wage, utility, and tax expenses during the fiscal year but, as of the fiscal year-end, had not yet paid for them in cash.

To summarize several important points about the income statement:

1. All revenues should eventually result in cash inflows to a business, and all expenses should at some point result in cash outflows. However, the recognition of revenues and expenses in the income statement has practically *nothing whatsoever* to do with the *timing* of the cash receipts or the cash disbursements.
2. Revenues that have been earned for which no cash has been received will cause accounts receivable to appear on the balance sheet. Expenses that have been incurred for which no cash has been disbursed will cause liabilities to appear on the balance sheet or an asset other than cash to decrease.
3. Every revenue and expense contained in a company's income statement will also affect the assets or liabilities of that company. The net income for the period will cause a like increase in the company's owners' equity. A net loss (wherein revenues are less than expenses) will cause a like decrease in owners' equity.

The method of income determination just described is known as the *accrual method* of accounting. It states that: all revenues are recognized when earned; all expenses are recognized when incurred. The accrual method is required for preparing external financial statements in accordance with generally accepted accounting principles. Because it is not possible to tell anything about a company's actual cash flow from its income statement, one *cannot* assume that if a company reports a substantial net income, it must also have substantially increased its cash balance. As we will discuss in subsequent chapters, it is not unusual for profitable companies, especially those whose sales volumes are growing, to be "short on cash."

STATEMENT OF RETAINED EARNINGS ILLUSTRATED

The final concept to be addressed in this chapter is that of *retained earnings*. In Illustration 2-1, we see that Corner Drugstore's retained earnings as of its first fiscal year-end were $3,900. We know from Illustration 2-2, however, that the drugstore's net income (earnings) was $5,400. We have stated that a company's owners' equity increases by the amount of its earnings for a given period. This increase is reflected on the balance sheet through a component of owners' equity called *retained earnings*. It would seem to make sense, then, for the amount of Corner Drugstore's retained earnings at March 31, 1979 to be identical to the amount of net income reflected in its income statement for the fiscal year ending on that date. This indeed would be true if the company had chosen to retain all of its earnings for the year rather than to distribute some of its earnings to the owners in the form of *dividends*. We can conclude that during its first fiscal year, Corner Drugstore paid dividends to its stockholders in an amount equal to the difference between its net income for the year of $5,400 and its increase in retained earnings during the year of $3,900; a difference of $1,500.

The $5,400 net income represents an increase in net assets (total assets less total liabilities) during the year. It cannot be assumed that *cash* increased by $5,400, but only that total assets increased by that amount in relation to total liabilities. The increase in net assets due to earnings can be reflected not only through an increase in cash, but through increases in accounts receivable, inventory, equipment, and other assets as well. There is no such thing as a "retained earnings vault" wherein a company keeps cash equivalent to the amount of retained earnings shown on its balance sheet. Those who have searched for the key to such a vault have been the victims of accounting mythology.

On the other hand, dividends to stockholders are usually paid in cash. The purpose of dividend payments is to distribute some of a corporation's cash generated from profitable operations (earnings) to the owners, thus providing them with a return on their investment in the corporation. In order to pay dividends, a company must have: (1) cash, and (2) retained earnings, both of which are equal to or greater in amount than the dividend payments.

The decision by a corporation to pay a dividend is the responsibility of its Board of Directors. If the Board decides to authorize a dividend payment, three chronological dates associated with the dividend take on particular significance. These are:

1. *Date of Declaration* This is the date of the Board's assertion that the company will pay a dividend. At this point the company incurs a liability for the dividend payment.
2. *Date of Record* This is the date used to determine the specific stockholders to receive the dividend. Whoever owns capital

stock on this date is entitled to receive a dividend equal to the number of shares of stock owned times the amount of the per share dividend.
3. *Date of Payment*   This is the date on which the cash dividend is paid to those stockholders who owned capital stock on the date of record.

Even though dividends represent cash disbursements, they are *not* an expense. They merely represent distribution to the owners of cash arising from corporate profits. Notice that dividends were not shown as an expense in the income statement and did not enter into the calculation of net income. Once the amount of net income has been determined, then the Board of Directors must decide how much should be "retained" and how much should be distributed to the owners in the form of cash dividends. Dividends can even be paid during years when a company reports a loss so long as the cash is available and the retained earnings balance exceeds the amount of the dividend.

To reconcile a corporation's retained earnings balance at the beginning of its fiscal year with its retained earnings balance at fiscal year-end, accountants prepare a third basic financial statement, the statement of retained earnings. Illustration 2-3 contains such a statement for the first fiscal year of Corner Drugstore.

Illustration 2-3

Corner Drugstore, Inc.
Statement of Retained Earnings
For the Fiscal Year Ended March 31, 1979

Retained earnings, March 31, 1978	$ 0
Add: Net income for the year	5,400
Total	5,400
Less: Cash dividends	1,500
Retained earnings, March 31, 1979	$3,900

Once again, let's consider the information provided by the heading of the statement.

1. WHO?   Corner Drugstore, Inc.
2. WHAT?   Statement of Retained Earnings
3. WHEN?   Fiscal Year Ended March 31, 1979

Like the income statement, the statement of retained earnings covers a *period of time*, usually a fiscal year. As mentioned earlier, corporations often combine the income statement and the statement of retained earnings into a single statement. A *statement of income and retained earnings* is illustrated in Chapter 3.

SUMMARY

For external reporting purposes, businesses have traditionally prepared three financial statements: the balance sheet, the income statement, and the statement of retained earnings. All three statements are based on the fundamental accounting equation:

$$\text{Assets (A)} = \text{Liabilities (L)} + \text{Owners' Equity (OE)}$$

The balance sheet presents the dollar amount of business assets, liabilities, and owners' equity at a specific point in time. The income statement presents business revenues and expenses during a specific period of time. The statement of retained earnings presents a summary of the changes in business retained earnings during a specified period of time.

The fourth basic financial statement, the statement of changes in financial position, will be discussed in detail in Chapter 4.

3

The Accounting Process

In this chapter, business events and transactions are defined, and the manner in which they are treated in a company's financial records is discussed. The double-entry system of accounting is described, and the procedures that comprise the accounting process, beginning with the initial recording of business transactions and ending with the preparation of financial statements, are illustrated.

In Chapter 2, we described the nature and purpose of the balance sheet and the statements of income and retained earnings. In this chapter, we will explain how these financial statements were derived. To do so, it will be necessary to consider everything that occurred between April 3, 1978 and March 31, 1979 that affected either the resources or obligations of Corner Drugstore. We will also describe the accounting procedures used by Corner Drugstore in recording, summarizing, and presenting the results of its first year's activities.

BUSINESS EVENTS

Business events can be divided into two classes: those that cause a company's financial position to change, and those that do not. Only those events that affect a company's financial position are given accounting recognition. We will refer to events of this type as *transactions*. Thus, business transactions affect the financial position of a company and must be recorded on a company's books and reflected in its financial statements.

Examples of common business transactions are the sale of capital stock, the purchase or sale of merchandise, and the purchase of equipment. Business events that do not affect a company's financial position (and therefore are not transactions) often take the form of *executory contracts*. These are agreements a company makes with one or more other companies or individuals, the terms which have not yet been fulfilled. No accounting recognition is given to executory contracts at the time they are made. As these contracts are fulfilled, appropriate accounting recognition occurs. Executory contracts include (1) employment agreements, (2) rental agreements, and (3) agreements to purchase or sell merchandise at a future time.

ACCOUNTS AND THE DOUBLE-ENTRY SYSTEM OF ACCOUNTING

As business transactions occur, their effects upon a company's assets, liabilities, and owners' equity are recorded on the books through the use of *accounts*. In its simplest form, an account resembles the letter "T" and is referred to as a *T-account*. Its purpose is to provide an easy means for recording the dollar amount of an increase or decrease in each individual asset, liability, or component of owners' equity. In a manual system, all of a company's accounts are bound together into a type of book called a *ledger*. Each page of the ledger contains a separate account, and each account represents a different balance sheet component, such as merchandise inventory or wages payable. Each T-account is divided in half by a vertical line drawn down the middle of the page. One side records the dollar amount of increases in the account; the other side records the dollar amount of account decreases. The *balance* of each account is determined by subtracting the total of the decrease side from the total of the increase side. The name of each account is placed at the top.

The double-entry system of accounting provides the basis for recording changes in account balances. The financial consequences of every transaction recorded by the double-entry system must result in equal amounts placed on the left side of some accounts and on the right side of other accounts. As a result, the sum of all accounts with left-side balances must always equal the sum of all the accounts with right-side balances. A ledger is said to be *in balance* when such a state of account balance equality exists. Illustration 3-1 contains the balances for each of Corner Drugstore's accounts as of the end of its first fiscal year.

As a practical matter, companies assign a number to each of their ledger accounts. Both the quantity of accounts and the numbering system will vary among businesses due to differences in such factors as the nature of the business, the size of the business, and the extent to which management desires detailed records to be kept. Accounts are numbered in ascending order and are usually arranged in the ledger in the order in which they appear in the financial statements. Balance sheet accounts are generally shown first, then income statement accounts. Small companies may need only two-digit numbers, whereas large companies may need four or more digits. The account numbering system is frequently designed so that the nature of each account (i.e., asset, liability, etc.) can be identified from the account number. Companies maintain a *chart of accounts* that consists of a complete listing of all their account titles and corresponding account numbers.

Rules for Entering Amounts in the Ledger Accounts

The increases in some accounts are recorded on the left side, whereas the increases in other accounts are recorded on the right side. The following conventions are prescribed under double-entry accounting:

Type of Account	How Recorded
Asset	Increases on the left; decreases on the right
Liability	Increases on the right; decreases on the left
Owners' Equity	Increases on the right; decreases on the left

Notice that asset increases are recorded on the left side of the account but that the opposite is true for liabilities and owners' equity. The logic of this inverse relationship can be explained through the accounting equation, $A = L + OE$. In any mathematical equation,

Illustration 3-1

Corner Drugstore, Inc.
Ledger Account Balances
March 31, 1979

Cash (A)
3-31-79 Balance	2,500

Accounts Receivable (A)
3-31-79 Balance	4,200

Merchandise Inventory (A)
3-31-79 Balance	12,700

Store Equipment (A)
(Original Cost $10,000) 3-31-79 Balance	9,000

Accounts Payable (L)
Balance 3-31-79	3,800

Wages Payable (L)
Balance 3-31-79	700

Utilities Payable (L)
Balance 3-31-79	200

Taxes Payable (L)
Balance 3-31-79	2,300

Bank Loan Payable (L)
Balance 3-31-79	7,500

Capital Stock (OE)
Balance 3-31-79	10,000

Retained Earnings (OE)
Balance 3-31-79	3,900

moving from one side of the equation to the other requires that the sign (+ or −) of the number be changed. Similarly, moving from one side of the accounting equation to the other requires that the manner of recording increases and decreases in accounts be reversed. Thus, the rules for recording changes in assets are just the opposite of those for recording changes in liabilities and owners' equity.

In summary, the rules of entering business transactions are as follows:

$$A = L + OE$$

Asset Accounts	
Increases	Decreases

Liability Accounts	
Decreases	Increases

Owners' Equity Accounts	
Decreases	Increases

ANALYSIS OF BUSINESS TRANSACTIONS

The analysis of any business transaction can be accomplished by answering the following four questions:

1. What accounts in the ledger are affected by the transaction?
2. What kind of accounts are these (A, L, or OE)?
3. Are the affected accounts increased or decreased by the transaction and by how much?
4. What are the "left-hand" and "right-hand" effects of the transaction according to the rules of double-entry accounting for entering transactions in the ledger accounts?

Let us illustrate the process by applying it to a transaction involving the purchase of $300 of merchandise on account by Corner Drugstore.

1. Accounts affected: Merchandise Inventory
       Accounts Payable

2. Kinds of accounts: Merchandise Inventory (A)
       Accounts Payable (L)

3. Accounts increased or decreased and by how much: Merchandise Inventory (A) increased $300
       Accounts Payable (L) increased $300

4. Left-hand and right-hand effects: Enter $300 on left side of Merchandise Inventory account
       Enter $300 on right side of Accounts Payable account

Illustration 3-2 shows the manner in which Corner Drugstore would

Illustration 3-2
Analysis of Transactions

Accounts Affected	Amount of Increase or Decrease			
	Left		Right	
(1)				
Merchandise Inventory (A)	Incr	300		
Accounts Payable (L)			Incr	300
(2)				
Accounts Receivable (A)	Incr	100		
Retained Earnings (OE)-(Sales)			Incr	100
(3)				
Accounts Payable (L)	Decr	300		
Cash (A)			Decr	300
(4)				
Cash (A)	Incr	100		
Accounts Receivable (A)			Decr	100

record the $300 merchandise purchase, as well as the three additional transactions described below. A *journal* is used by businesses to record business transactions chronologically as they occur. The form for making entries in a journal is somewhat similar to that used in Illustration 3-2. In this text, we shall refer to the process of recording transactions on a company's books as the *analysis of transactions*.

The other transactions appearing in Illustration 3-2 are:

Transaction 2: The drugstore sold for $100 merchandise costing $60. The sale was "on account." (Notice that at the time of sale, the sale but not the cost of the goods sold is recorded. The cost of the merchandise sold is recorded at year-end, as we will discuss later in this chapter.)

Transaction 3: The drugstore paid for the merchandise previously purchased.

Transaction 4: The drugstore collected its account receivable of $100.

The generally accepted form associated with the analysis of transactions requires that:

1. The left-hand portion of each entry is shown first.
2. The right-hand portion is indented to the right of the left-hand portion.
3. Each account is given the exact title it has in the ledger.
4. An entry affecting the Retained Earnings account includes a brief parenthetical explanation so that when the entry is made in the Retained Earnings account in the ledger, the explanation can also be shown there.

CORNER DRUGSTORE'S TRANSACTIONS FOR ONE YEAR

Let us now go behind the financial statements presented in Chapter 2, and at the same time further illustrate the analysis of transactions by recording Corner Drugstore's transactions for its first fiscal year. These are actually *summary transactions* because we have grouped all similar transactions that occurred throughout the year and will record only the yearly totals. For example, Transaction C of Illustration 3-3 reflects the total merchandise purchased by the drugstore on account throughout the entire fiscal year. Keep in mind that on the company's books, each purchase of merchandise would be recorded separately and chronologically in its journal. In Illustration 3-3, each summary transaction described is immediately followed by an analysis of the transaction. For ease of illustration, all payroll taxes have been omitted from the Corner Drugstore example.

It is now possible for us to derive the individual account balances for Corner Drugstore as of March 31, 1979 that were presented in Illustration 3-1. All that we need to do is establish a separate account for each specific asset, liability, and component of owners' equity; enter the balance in each account as of the beginning of the 1979 fiscal year (which was $0 in every case since 1979 was the first year of operations); record each transaction in the appropriate accounts; and determine each account's fiscal year-end balance. The results are shown in Illustration 3-4. Before continuing, *trace all of the transactions in Illustration 3-3 to the accounts listed in Illustration 3-4.*

The following important characteristics of a company's ledger accounts are illustrated by those of Corner Drugstore in Illustration 3-4:

1. Balance sheet accounts carry forward from year to year, with the dollar amount of the fiscal year-end balance becoming the

Illustration 3-3

Corner Drugstore, Inc.
Analysis of Summary Transactions
Fiscal Year Ended March 31, 1979

Transaction A: Issued capital stock to the two incorporators in exchange for $10,000 cash.

Cash (A)	Incr	10,000		
Capital Stock (OE)			Incr	10,000

Event B: Signed a three-year lease on the building in which the drugstore was to be located. The lease called for a monthly rental of $300 and was cancellable by either the lessor or the lessee (Corner Drugstore) upon at least sixty days advance notice.

    No entry for Event B

This business event does not affect the financial resources or obligations of Corner Drugstore. Even though the drugstore signed the lease, the agreement is an executory contract that has yet to be performed. Corner Drugstore does not incur a liability to the lessor until the lease period occurs and the drugstore uses the building. At the time the lease is signed, no assets or liabilities are affected and no amounts are recorded in any of the drugstore's account. Thus, no "transaction analysis" is needed.

Transaction C: Purchased merchandise in the amount of $57,400 all on credit. (Payment was usually due within 30 days of the purchase date.)

Merchandise Inventory (A)	Incr	57,400		
Accounts Payable (L)			Incr	57,400

Transaction D: Borrowed $9,000 from a local bank on April 4, 1978. Repayment was to be made in six annual amounts, beginning on March 31, 1979. Interest of 5 percent per year on the unpaid balance was also due on that same date each year.

Cash (A)	Incr	9,000		
Bank Loan Payable (L)			Incr	9,000

Transaction E: Purchased store equipment for a total of $10,000 cash.

Store Equipment (A)	Incr	10,000		
Cash (A)			Decr	10,000

Transaction F: Cash sales amounted to $30,300.

Cash (A)	Incr	30,300		
Retained Earnings (OE) − (Cash Sales)			Incr	30,300

Transaction G: Credit sales amounted to $45,500.

Accounts Receivable (A)	Incr	45,500		
Retained Earnings (OE) − (Credit Sales)			Incr	45,500

Transaction H: Customers returned merchandise that they previously had purchased in the amount of $1,300. Of this, $500 had been cash sales and $800 had been credit sales.

Retained Earnings (OE) − (Sales Returns)	Decr	1,300		
Cash (A)			Decr	500
Accounts Receivable (A)			Decr	800

Transaction I: Collections of accounts receivable totaled $40,500.

Cash (A)	Incr	40,500		
Accounts Receivable (A)			Decr	40,500

Transaction J: Payments for merchandise previously purchased on credit amounted to $53,600.

Accounts Payable (L)	Decr	53,600		
Cash (A)			Decr	53,600

Transaction K: Paid cash for rent totaling $3,600. This amount is the total rent due to the owner of the building for its use for the entire year.

    Retained Earnings (OE) – (Rent)   Decr   3,600
    Cash (A)   Decr   3,600

Transaction L: Paid cash wages to employees totaling $14,600. As of March 31, 1979, wages earned by employees but not yet paid were $700.

    Retained Earnings (OE) – (Wages)   Decr   15,300
    Cash (A)   Decr   14,600
    Wages Payable (L)   Incr   700

Transaction M: Paid cash for utilities in the amount of $450. As of March 31, 1979, Corner Drugstore owed an additional $200 for utilities.

    Retained Earnings (OE) – (Utilities)   Decr   650
    Cash (A)   Decr   450
    Utilities Payable (L)   Incr   200

Transaction N: Estimated federal and state income taxes paid during the year amounted to $600. At fiscal year-end, an additional tax of $2,300 was due on the income actually earned during the year, suggesting that the drugstore was more profitable during its first year than the owners expected.

    Retained Earnings (OE) – (Income Taxes)   Decr   2,900
    Cash (A)   Decr   600
    Income Taxes Payable (L)   Incr   2,300

Transaction O: Paid cash for "other expenses" in the amount of $500.

    Retained Earnings (OE) – (Other Expenses)   Decr   500
    Cash (A)   Decr   500

Transaction P: On March 31, paid the first installment due on the bank loan, totaling $1,950. Of this amount, $1,500 was repayment of the principal, and $450 was interest expense.

    Bank Loan Payable (L)   Decr   1,500
    Retained Earnings (OE) – (Interest)   Decr   450
    Cash (A)   Decr   1,950

Transaction Q: $1,000 of the original cost of the store equipment was "written-off" the balance sheet and allocated to expense. An expense of this type is known as "depreciation."

    Retained Earnings (OE) – (Depreciation)   Decr   1,000
    Store Equipment   Decr   1,000

Transaction R: The cost to corner Drugstore of the merchandise that was sold and not returned during the year totaled $44,700.

    Retained Earnings (OE) – (Cost of
        Merchandise Sold)   Decr   44,700
    Merchandise Inventory (A)   Decr   44,700

Transaction S: Cash dividends of $1,500 were declared and paid.

    At date of declaration:
        Retained Earnings (OE) – (Dividends)   Decr   1,500
        Dividends Payable (L)   Incr   1,500

    At date of payment:
        Dividends Payable (L)   Decr   1,500
        Cash (A)   Decr   1,500

Illustration 3-4

Transactions Entered in Corner Drugstore's Ledger
Fiscal Year Ended March 31, 1979

Cash (A)

3-31-78 Balance	-0-	(E)	10,000
(A)	10,000	(H)	500
(D)	9,000	(J)	53,600
(F)	30,300	(K)	3,600
(I)	40,500	(L)	14,600
		(M)	450
		(N)	600
		(O)	500
		(P)	1,950
		(S)	1,500
			87,300
		To balance	2,500
	89,800		89,800
3-31-79 Balance	2,500		

Accounts Receivable (A)

3-31-78 Balance	-0-	(H)	800
(G)	45,500	(I)	40,500
			41,300
		To balance	4,200
	45,500		45,500
3-31-79 Balance	4,200		

Merchandise Inventory (A)

3-31-78 Balance	-0-	(R)	44,700
(C)	57,400		
			44,700
		To balance	12,700
	57,400		57,400
3-31-79 Balance	12,700		

Store Equipment (A)

3-31-78 Balance	-0-	(Q)	1,000
(E)	10,000		
			1,000
		To balance	9,000
	10,000		10,000
3-31-79 Balance	9,000		

The Accounting Process

Accounts Payable (L)

(J)	53,600	3-31-78 Balance	-0-
		(C)	57,400
	53,600		
To balance	3,800		
	57,400		57,400
		3-31-79 Balance	3,800

Wages Payable (L)

To balance	700	3-31-78 Balance	-0-
		(L)	700
		3-31-79 Balance	700

Utilities Payable (L)

		3-31-78 Balance	-0-
To balance	200	(M)	200
		3-31-79 Balance	200

Taxes Payable (L)

		3-31-78 Balance	-0-
To balance	2,300	(N)	2,300
		3-31-79 Balance	2,300

Bank Loan Payable (L)

(P)	1,500	3-31-78 Balance	-0-
		(D)	9,000
	1,500		
To balance	7,500		
	9,000		9,000
		3-31-79 Balance	7,500

Dividends Payable (L)

(S)	1,500	3-31-78 Balance	-0-
		(S)	1,500
		3-31-79 Balance	-0-

Capital Stock (OE)

To balance	10,000	4-1-78 Balance (A)	-0- 10,000
		3-31-79 Balance	10,000

Retained Earnings (OE)

(H) Sales returns	1,300	3-31-78 Balance	-0-
(K) Rent expense	3,600	(F) Cash sales	30,300
(L) Wages expense	15,300	(G) Credit sales	45,500
(M) Utilities expense	650		
(N) Taxes expense	2,900		
(O) Other expenses	500		
(P) Interest expense	450		
(Q) Depreciation expense	1,000		
(R) Cost of merchandise sold	44,700		
(S) Dividends	1,500		
	71,900		
To balance	3,900		
	75,800		75,800
		3-31-79 Balance	3,900

dollar amount of the account balance at the beginning of the new fiscal year.
2. Sometimes the year-end balance of an account is zero.
3. All revenues cause retained earnings to increase. All expenses and all contra-revenues (such as sales returns) cause retained earnings to decrease.
4. All of the data needed to prepare an income statement and a retained earnings statement are contained in the retained earnings account. Each entry to retained earnings must be identified to facilitate these statements' preparation.
5. Not all of the entries in the retained earnings account pertain to transactions affecting the income statement. For example, transaction S pertaining to cash dividends decreased retained earnings, yet dividends are not an expense and therefore do not affect the calculation of net income.

TRIAL BALANCE

Now that we have determined the balance in each ledger account as of March 31, 1979, we need to make sure that the total of the left-hand account balances equals the total of the right-hand account balances. We know that this equality existed as of the beginning of the first fiscal year (all balances were zero), and we attempted to record each transaction so that equal left-hand and right-hand entries were made. Therefore, we can be reasonably confident that at year-end the ledger accounts are *in balance*; that is, total left-hand and right-hand balances are equal.

To prove the company's ledger is in balance, we will prepare a *trial balance*. From the one presented in Illustration 3-5, we can see that:

1. Accounts are listed on the trial balance in the same order that they appear on the balance sheet.
2. No dollar signs are used because the trial balance is not an actual financial statement, just a convenient means of proving that the ledger accounts are in balance.
3. The trial balance proves only the mathematical equality of the left-hand and right-hand entries in the accounts. The trial

Illustration 3-5

Corner Drugstore, Inc.
Trial Balance
March 31, 1979

Account Name	Left-Hand Balance	Right-Hand Balance
Cash	2,500	
Accounts Receivable	4,200	
Merchandise Inventory	12,700	
Store Equipment (Cost $10,000)	9,000	
Accounts Payable		3,800
Wages Payable		700
Utilities Payable		200
Taxes Payable		2,300
Bank Loan Payable		7,500
Dividends Payable		-0-
Capital Stock		10,000
Retained Earnings		3,900
Total	28,400	28,400

balance does not prove that the transactions were properly analyzed or that they were entered in the proper accounts.

THE REPORT FORM OF BALANCE SHEET

We are now ready to prepare the basic financial statements of Corner Drugstore. In Chapter 2, we illustrated the *account form* of balance sheet. Several other forms of balance sheet presentation are also used by businesses. Illustration 3-6 presents Corner Drugstore's March 31, 1979 balance sheet in the *report form*, wherein liabilities and owners' equity are shown below assets. A variation of the report form shows a downward sequence of total assets minus total liabilities equal to total owners' equity. Another form used occasionally is the *financial position form*. This form of balance sheet shows current assets less current liabilities equal to working capital (net current assets). Noncurrent assets are then added and noncurrent liabilities deducted

---

Illustration 3-6

Corner Drugstore, Inc.
Balance Sheet
March 31, 1979

Assets

Cash	$ 2,500
Accounts receivable	4,200
Merchandise inventory	12,700
Store equipment (cost $10,000)	9,000
Total assets	28,400

Liabilities and Owners' Equity

Accounts payable		3,800
Wages payable		700
Utilities payable		200
Income taxes payable		2,300
Bank loan payable		7,500
Total liabilities		14,500
Capital stock	$10,000	
Retained earnings	3,900	13,900
Total liabilities and owners' equity		$28,400

The Accounting Process

from working capital to arrive at the total amount of net assets (total assets less total liabilities). Owners' equity is shown last, the total of which is equal to the amount of the net assets. The balance sheet of Caterpillar Tractor Company illustrated in subsequent chapters is an example of the *financial position form*.

COMBINED STATEMENT OF INCOME AND RETAINED EARNINGS

In Chapter 2, we mentioned that the income statement and the statement of retained earnings are often combined into a single statement. This combination is possible because both statements cover the same period of time and because both statements reflect

---

Illustration 3-7

Corner Drugstore, Inc.
Statement of Income and Retained Earnings
For the Fiscal Year Ended March 31, 1979

Gross sales		$75,800
Less: Sales returns		1,300
Net sales		74,500
Less: Cost of merchandise sold		44,700
Gross margin on sales		29,800
Less Operating expenses:		
Employees wages	$15,300	
Rent	3,600	
Utilities	650	
Allocated cost of store equipment	1,000	
Other	500	
Total operating expenses		21,050
Income from operations		8,750
Less: Interest on bank loan		450
Income before income taxes		8,300
Less: Federal and state income taxes		2,900
Net income		5,400
Add: Retained earnings, March 31, 1978		-0-
		5,400
Less: Cash dividends		1,500
Retained earnings, March 31, 1979		$ 3,900

transactions affecting retained earnings. Illustration 3-7 contains a combined statement of income and retained earnings for Corner Drugstore's first fiscal year prepared solely from the data provided by the retained earnings ledger account in Illustration 3-4.

COMPARATIVE FINANCIAL STATEMENTS

Companies customarily provide external users of their financial statements with information pertaining to more than one fiscal year through the preparation of comparative financial statements. A comparative balance sheet shows a company's financial position as of two or more consecutive fiscal year-ends. A comparative statement of income and retained earnings presents the results of a company's activities during two or more consecutive fiscal years.

Representative comparative financial statements for Corner Drug-

Illustration 3-8

Corner Drugstore, Inc.
Comparative Balance Sheet
March 31, 1980 and March 31, 1979

Assets	3/31/80	3/31/79
Cash	$ 575	$ 2,500
Accounts receivable	7,400	4,200
Merchandise inventory	18,000	12,700
Store equipment (cost $15,000; $10,000)	12,500	9,000
Total assets	38,475	28,400
Liabilities and Owners' Equity		
Accounts payable	6,200	3,800
Wages payable	900	700
Utilities payable	100	200
Income taxes payable	1,800	2,300
Bank loan payable	6,000	7,500
Total liabilities	15,000	14,500
Capital stock	13,000	10,000
Retained earnings	10,475	3,900
Total liabilities and owners' equity	$38,475	$28,400

Illustration 3-9

Corner Drugstore, Inc.
Comparative Statement of Income and Retained Earnings
For the Fiscal Years Ended March 31, 1980 and March 31, 1979

		1980		1979
Gross sales		$103,700		$75,800
Less: Sales returns		3,200		1,300
Net sales		100,500		74,500
Less: Cost of merchandise sold		60,300		44,700
Gross margin on sales		40,200		29,800
Less Operating expenses:				
Employees wages	$18,500		$15,300	
Rent	3,600		3,600	
Utilities	850		650	
Depreciation of				
store equipment	1,500		1,000	
Other	750		500	
Total operating expenses		25,200		21,050
Income from operations		15,000		8,750
Less: Interest on bank loan		375		450
Income before income taxes		14,625		8,300
Less: Federal and state income taxes		6,050		2,900
Net income		8,575		5,400
Add: Beginning retained earnings		3,900		-0-
		12,475		5,400
Less: Cash dividends		2,000		1,500
Ending retained earnings		$ 10,475		$ 3,900

store for its 1980 and 1979 fiscal years are shown in Illustrations 3-8 and 3-9. A summary of the drugstore's transactions for its fiscal year ended March 31, 1980 is intentionally omitted from this chapter for reasons that will become evident in Chapter 4.

REMARKS ABOUT THE APPROACH

At this point in the development of accounting fundamentals, we wish to distinguish between the manner in which we have presented certain aspects of the accounting process and the more traditional method of presentation. The first such difference pertains to the recording of amounts in the ledger accounts. In our discussion, we stated that each account has a left-side and a right-side, and that accountants have developed rules requiring that changes in asset accounts be recorded in a manner opposite from changes in liability and owners' equity accounts. The more traditional presentation of changes in account balances introduces the terms "debit" and "credit." Notwithstanding that these terms are part of the accounting language, we avoid their use for two reasons. First, preconceived notions about these terms are often wrong and are very difficult to change. Second, debit means nothing more than the left side of an account, and credit means nothing more than the right side of an account. Omitting their use gives up little in terms of substance but avoids a considerable amount of confusion.

Another difference between our presentation and a more traditional one pertains to the retained earnings account. Whereas we recorded all of Corner Drugstore's revenues and expenses directly in its retained earnings account, the more traditional method (and the one actually used by businesses) establishes separate accounts for each revenue and for each expense. The net difference between the revenues and the expenses is then recorded periodically in the retained earnings account.

As we have presented it, then, the *accounting process* can be described as follows:

1. Transactions are identified and chronologically recorded in a journal through an analysis of transactions.
2. Periodically, the chronologically recorded data are entered in the appropriate ledger accounts. These entries are made at least every fiscal year-end.
3. A trial-balance is prepared to prove the mathematical equality of the left-hand and right-hand balances in the ledger accounts.
4. The basic financial statements are prepared.

SUMMARY

Business financial records are kept in accordance with the requirements of the double-entry system of accounting. The account is used to collect financial information about business transactions. Each account has a left side and a right side, and the rules are such that increases in assets are recorded in the left side of an account whereas decreases in assets are recorded in the right side of an account. The reverse is true for recording changes in liabilities and owners' equity. Prior to the preparation of financial statements, a trial balance is prepared to make sure that the total of the left-hand account balance is equal to the total of the right-hand account balance. Comparative financial statements for two or more years are usually prepared for external reporting purposes.

4

Statement of Changes in Financial Position

For external reporting purposes, the presentation of a statement of changes in financial position has been required only since 1971. This chapter is devoted primarily to the illustration and discussion of the preparation and purpose of this new and informative financial statement. The latter part of this chapter addresses some of the limitations of all of the basic financial statements.

With the issuance of Accounting Principles Board (APB) Opinion No. 19 in March 1971, the accounting profession adopted the *statement of changes in financial position* as a basic financial statement that must be presented whenever financial statements purporting to disclose both financial position and results of operations are made available to external users. The APB believed that this statement would provide additional relevant financial information useful in making economic decisions.

The belief that a financial statement disclosing all significant changes in a company's financial position would be externally useful dates back to the development of a "where-got, where-gone" statement by William M. Cole in the early 1900s. Then about 1920, an accounting educator and author named H. A. Finney advocated that a financial statement entitled the "statement of sources and uses of funds" be a required financial statement for external reporting purposes. Whereas Cole's financial statement disclosed changes in all balance sheet accounts, Finney's financial statement discussed only changes in a company's working capital position. *Working capital* is defined as the excess of a company's *current assets* over its *current liabilities*. In equation form, this relationship is:

$$\text{Working Capital} = \text{Current Assets} - \text{Current Liabilities}$$

or

$$W.C. = C.A. - C.L.$$

Current assets are cash and other assets that normally will be converted into cash or sold or consumed within one year from the date of the balance sheet. *Current liabilities* are debts or obligations due within one year of the balance sheet date. Current assets include cash, accounts receivable, and inventory; current liabilities include accounts payable, wages payable, and the current portion due of any long-term obligation.

A company's working capital position is generally regarded as a measure of the company's ability to meet its short-term financial obligations, that is, those obligations due within the next year. Finney's statement of sources and uses of funds, where "funds" meant "working capital," was an early predecessor to the statement of changes in financial position required by APB Opinion No. 19.

THE STATEMENT'S FORM AND CONTENT

The statement of changes in financial position summarizes *all* significant *changes* that have occurred between the beginning and end of a company's accounting period (generally a fiscal year for external reporting purposes). In accordance with APB Opinion No. 19, the statement must:

1. Be based on a broad concept embracing all significant changes in financial position.
2. Prominently disclose *either* working capital *or* cash provided from or used in operations for the period.
3. Begin with income or loss and add back (or deduct) items recognized in determining that income or loss that did not use or provide working capital or cash during the period.
4. Disclose, either on the statement or a related tabulation, the net changes in each element of working capital (i.e., each current asset and current liability) for the period.

Within these guidelines, companies are permitted considerable flexibility in the statement's preparation. In each case, management should adopt the presentation that is most informative for the circumstances.

Although Opinion No. 19 permits the statement of changes in financial position to be prepared so as to disclose either changes in working capital or changes in cash, most companies choose the "working capital" format. We believe that much of the popularity of disclosure of working capital changes over disclosure of cash changes is due to the accounting profession's familiarity with H. A. Finney's "working capital-based" funds statement. There are indications, however, that the "cash-based" funds statement may increase in popularity during the 1980s due to the increased importance of cash flow analysis.

PREPARATION OF THE STATEMENT

Regardless of whether the statement is prepared to disclose working capital changes or cash changes, it is based on data obtained from a company's comparative balance sheet, its current year's statement of income and retained earnings, and from various internal accounting records. Thus, much of what is contained in the statement of changes in financial position could be extracted by external users from the other basic financial statements. Its real values, then, are its disclosure of data not found on the other statements and the manner in which it presents a company's significant financial changes.

In this chapter, we address only the preparation of the statement of changes in financial position designed to disclose changes in *working capital*. We do so, first, because the working capital approach is most commonly used and, second, because the disclosure of significant changes in cash will be discussed in Chapter 5. From the data presented in Illustration 3-8 and 3-9, we will complete the Corner Drugstore's set of basic financial statements by preparing a statement of changes in financial position for the fiscal year ending March 31, 1980.

A statement of changes in financial position prepared on the working capital basis has three major objectives. These are:

1. To disclose the manner in which a company's working capital position changed during the period. Thus, the statement lists all *working capital accounts* (i.e., all current assets and current liabilities), their balances at the beginning and end of the period, and the effect that each of these account balance changes had on the company's working capital position. Such a listing is often called a *schedule of working changes* and usually appears at the bottom of or as an attachment to the statement of changes in financial position.
2. To disclose the *reasons* for the change in a company's working capital position.
3. To disclose all other significant changes in financial position that did not affect working capital, citing the reasons for these changes. (Corner Drugstore did not have any such changes.)

To summarize, the primary goal of the statement of changes in financial position is to report all financially significant changes in a company's financial position that occurred during the period covered by the statement and to disclose the causes of these changes. In a working capital-based statement, the changes in financial position are organized into two categories: changes that affected working capital, and changes that did not. (Corner Drugstore had no changes in the second category.)

The first step in preparing the statement is to determine the amount by which Corner Drugstore's working capital position changed during its 1980 fiscal year. We do so by developing the schedule of working capital changes shown in Illustration 4-1. The right-hand column shows the *effects* on *working capital* of the changes in each current asset and current liability account balance. Notice that increases

Illustration 4-1

Corner Drugstore, Inc.
Schedule of Working Capital Changes
For the Fiscal Year Ended March 31, 1980

	Balance 3/31/80	Balance 3/31/79	Working Capital Incr. or (Decr.)
Current Assets:			
Cash	$ 575	$ 2,500	$(1,925)
Accounts receivable	7,400	4,200	3,200
Merchandise inventory	18,000	12,700	5,300
	25,975	19,400	6,575
Current Liabilities:			
Accounts payable	6,200	3,800	(2,400)
Wages payable	900	700	(200)
Utilities payable	100	200	100
Taxes payable	1,800	2,300	500
Bank loan payable (current)	1,500	1,500	-0-
	10,500	8,500	(2,000)
Working Capital	$15,475	$10,900	$ 4,575

in current assets increase working capital; decreases in current assets decrease working capital. The reverse is true, however, for current liabilities. Increases in current liabilities cause working capital to decrease; decreases in current liabilities cause working capital to increase. The logic of these relationships is based on the definition of working capital: W.C. = C.A. − C.L. A direct relationship exists between changes in current assets and changes in working capital. An inverse relationship exists between changes in current liabilities and changes in working capital.

Now that we have determined that during the 1980 fiscal year the working capital for Corner Drugstore increased by $4,575, our next step is to prepare a statement of changes in financial position for the purpose of explaining what caused the increase. The fundamental concept underlying the statement's preparation, although not particularly difficult, is somewhat elusive and requires considerable thought. The only way to determine what caused a change in a company's working capital position is to analyze the changes in all of the company's *nonworking capital accounts*. Nonworking capital accounts are all accounts *other than* the current assets and current liabilities. Changes in current accounts establish the *amount* and *direction* of a change in working capital. Changes in noncurrent accounts reveal the *reasons* for the change in working capital.

To analyze changes in a company's nonworking capital accounts means examining each such account to determine the specific cause of every increase or decrease recorded in the account throughout the reporting period. The specific reasons for changes in the noncurrent accounts must be identified, because *every transaction that causes a company's working capital position to change also causes the balance in one or more of a company's noncurrent accounts to change by an equal amount*. Therefore, a transaction must affect both a current and a noncurrent account to affect working capital. Transactions affecting only current accounts have *no* effect whatsoever on working capital. Similarly, transactions affecting only noncurrent accounts have *no* effect on working capital. Perhaps the best way to explain these ideas is to describe several different types of business transactions, to analyze them, and to test the results against the rationale just described.

Because an analysis of nonworking capital accounts entails identifying the specific causes of all significant increases or decreases in their balances, it is helpful to become familiar with some of the common transactions that affect the typical noncurrent accounts found on the balance sheets of most corporations. Some examples are as follows:

Nonworking Capital Account	Type of Account	Common Causes of Changes in the Account Balance
Machinery and Equipment	Asset	Acquistion Sale or disposal Depreciation
Long-Term Debt	Liability	Incur additional debt Repay debt Portion of long-term debt becomes current (due within the next year)
Capital Stock	Owners' Equity	Sell additional stock Purchase and retire existing stock
Retained Earnings	Owners' Equity	Net income or loss Dividends

We are now ready to examine all of Corner Drugstore's noncurrent accounts so that we can prepare its statement of changes in financial position. From the comparative balance sheet presented in Illustration 3-8, we can identify the noncurrent accounts as Store Equipment, the noncurrent portion of the Bank Loan Payable, Capital Stock, and Retained Earnings. Identifying the transactions affecting the balances in these four noncurrent accounts will provide us all the information needed to prepare the Corner Drugstore's statement of changes in financial position.

RECONSTRUCTION OF ACCOUNTS

The easiest way to identify the transactions affecting a company's noncurrent accounts is to gain access to the company's ledger and to observe the individual changes that occurred in these accounts during the period. Without such access, it is usually possible to reconstruct the activity in each noncurrent account by applying transaction analysis to the data provided by a company's comparative balance sheet and its combined statement of income and retained earnings.

We mentioned earlier in the chapter that, according to APB Opinion No. 19, the statement of changes in financial position should begin with the company's income. The net income figure must then be adjusted to eliminate the effects of any revenues or expenses that did not alter working capital. The logical place to start our reconstruction of accounts, then, is with an analysis of the retained earnings account. Illustration 4-2 was prepared solely from the data contained in Illustrations 3-8 and 3-9.

Because the difference between the left and right-side amounts in our reconstructed retained earnings account agrees with its 3-31-80 balance, we know that we have not omitted anything in our reconstruction. In other words, nothing affected retained earnings during the fiscal year other than net income and dividends, both of which

Illustration 4-2

Corner Drugstore, Inc.
Reconstruction of Retained Earnings Account
For the Fiscal Year Ended March 31, 1980

Retained Earnings

Dividends for the year	2,000	3-31-79 Balance	3,900
		Net income for the year	8,575
		3-31-80 Balance	10,475

Illustration 4-3

Corner Drugstore, Inc.
Reconstruction of Three Accounts
For the Fiscal Year Ended March 31, 1980

Store Equipment

3-31-79 Balance	9,000	Depreciation for the year	1,500
Plug	5,000		
3-31-80 Balance	12,500		

Bank Loan Payable (Noncurrent portion)

Plug	1,500	3-31-79 Balance	6,000
		3-31-80 Balance	4,500

Capital Stock

		3-31-79 Balance	10,000
		Plug	3,000
		3-31-80 Balance	13,000

are shown in our account reconstruction.

Once again using the financial information from Illustrations 3-8 and 3-9, we prepared a reconstruction of the other three noncurrent accounts of Corner Drugstore. The results are shown in Illustration 4-3.

Unlike the retained earnings account reconstruction, our reconstruction of the remaining three noncurrent accounts requires a "plug" figure to reach the 3-31-80 balances in the accounts. Each plug figure represents *one or more transactions* that occurred during the year and affected the account balance, the substance of which could *not* be obtained from the data presented in Illustrations 3-8 and 3-9. We must therefore apply some business logic.

The $5,000 plug figure in the store equipment account is a left-side entry, so we know that something occurred during the year to increase this account balance. We can conclude that the cost of equipment acquired exceeded the cost of the equipment disposed of by $5,000.

The $1,500 plug figure in the bank loan payable (noncurrent portion) account is also a left-side entry, but in this case it represents a transaction that reduced the long-term liability. This reduction can only be explained by a principal payment to the bank in the amount of $1,500 or by the reclassification of this amount from a noncurrent liability to a current liability.

In the case of the capital stock account, the $3,000 plug figure represents a transaction that caused this account balance to increase. The increase is explicable only by the issuance of additional capital stock in the amount of $3,000.

A SINGLE YEAR'S STATEMENT ILLUSTRATED

We can now prepare a statement of changes in financial position for Corner Drugstore for its 1980 fiscal year. Illustration 4-4 contains this statement prepared in accordance with the requirements set forth in APB Opinion No. 19.

The most difficult process to understand in Illustration 4-4 is undoubtedly the addition of depreciation to net income to reach the amount of working capital provided by operations. The net income figure of $8,575 represents the excess of Corner Drugstore's revenues over its expenses for the 1980 fiscal year. This amount is treated as a source of working capital because almost all revenues cause working capital to increase (through the receipt of cash or accounts receivable), and almost all expenses cause working capital to decrease (through the payment of cash or incurrence of a current liability).

If a company earns a revenue that does not increase working capital or incurs expenses that do not decrease working capital, the net income figure in the income statement does not represent the net change in working capital resulting from operations. To determine the true change, we must deduct from the net income figure any "nonworking capital" revenues, and add to it any "nonworking capital" expenses. Corner Drugstore had no such revenues and only one such expense—depreciation. When the drugstore recorded its depreciation expense of $1,500 for fiscal 1980, the two accounts affected were Store Equipment and Retained Earnings. Because neither of these is a current account, working capital was unaffected. Thus, depreciation represents a "nonworking capital" expense that must be added back

Illustration 4-4

Corner Drugstore, Inc.
Statement of Changes in Financial Position
For the Fiscal Year Ended March 31, 1980

Sources of Working Capital:

Net income	$ 8,575	
Add: Depreciation	1,500	
Working capital provided from operations	10,075	
Other sources of working capital:		
Issuance of capital stock	3,000	
Total sources of working capital		$13,075

Uses of Working Capital:

Payment of bank loan installment	1,500	
Purchase of store equipment (in excess of dispositions)	5,000	
Payment of dividends	2,000	
Total uses of working capital		8,500
Increase in working capital		$ 4,575

Schedule of working capital changes:

	Balance 3-31-80	Balance 3-31-79	Working Capital Incr. or (Decr.)
Current Assets:			
Cash	575	2,500	(1,925)
Accounts receivable	7,400	4,200	3,200
Merchandise inventory	18,000	12,700	5,300
	25,975	19,400	6,575
Current Liabilities:			
Accounts payable	6,200	3,800	(2,400)
Wages payable	900	700	(200)
Utilities payable	100	200	100
Taxes payable	1,800	2,300	500
Bank loan payable (current)	1,500	1,500	-0-
	10,500	8,500	(2,000)
Working Capital	$15,475	$10,900	$ 4,575

to net income to arrive at the amount of *working capital* actually provided from operations.

A COMPARATIVE STATEMENT ILLUSTRATED

Companies customarily publish comparative statements of changes in financial position. A comparative statement for Corner Drugstore

Statement of Changes in Financial Position 61

for its 1979 and 1980 fiscal years is presented in Illustration 4-5.

The only new item introduced by the fiscal 1979 statement of changes in financial position is the $7,500 source of working capital from the long-term bank loan. Because we know from previous chapters that the amount of the loan was $9,000, it may seem strange that working capital increased by only $7,500. The reason for this discrepancy lies in the terms of the loan. The loan agreement required

Illustration 4-5

Corner Drugstore, Inc.
Statement of Changes in Financial Position
For the Fiscal Years Ended March 31, 1980 and March 31, 1979

	1980	1979
Sources of Working Capital:		
Net income	$ 8,575	$ 5,400
Add: Depreciation	1,500	1,000
Working capital provided from operations	10,075	6,400
Other sources of working capital:		
Issuance of capital stock	3,000	10,000
Proceeds from bank loan		7,500
Total sources of working capital	$13,075	$23,900
Uses of Working Capital:		
Purchase of store equipment (in excess of dispositions)	5,000	10,000
Payment of dividends	2,000	1,500
Payment of bank loan installment	1,500	1,500
Total uses of working capital	8,500	13,000
Increase in working capital	$ 4,575	$10,900

Schedule of working capital changes:	Balance 3-31-80	Balance 3-31-79	Balance 3-31-78	1980 Working Capital Incr. or (Decr.)	1979 Working Capital Incr. or (Decr.)
Current Assets:					
Cash	$ 575	$ 2,500	-0-	$(1,925)	$ 2,500
Accounts receivable	7,400	4,200	-0-	3,200	4,200
Merchandise inventory	18,000	12,700	-0-	5,300	12,700
	25,975	19,400	-0-	6,575	19,400
Current Liabilities:					
Accounts payable	6,200	3,800	-0-	(2,400)	(3,800)
Wages payable	900	700	-0-	(200)	(700)
Utilities payable	100	200	-0-	100	(200)
Taxes payable	1,800	2,300	-0-	500	(2,300)
Bank loan payable (current)	1,500	1,500	-0-	-0-	(1,500)
	$10,500	$ 8,500	-0-	(2,000)	(8,500)
Change in Working Capital				$ 4,575	$10,900

that repayment be made in six installments beginning on March 31, 1979. The $1,500 amount of the principal repayment due in 1979 represented a *current* liability at the time the loan was granted. Therefore, the $9,000 cash received from the bank gave rise to a corresponding long-term liability of $7,500 and a current liability of $1,500. The net result was an increase in working capital (net current assets) of $9,000 minus $1,500, or $7,500.

LIMITATIONS OF EXTERNAL FINANCIAL STATEMENTS

Having discussed and illustrated all of the basic financial statements presented annually to external users, it is useful to indicate the limitations of such financial reports and to illustrate these limitations by referring to Corner Drugstore's statements.

1. The statements reflect only those transactions that have been accorded accounting recognition.

    According to generally accepted accounting principles, transactions given accounting recognition *exclude* sales backlogs, authorized future expenditures, contracts signed but not yet executed, accumulated customer goodwill, and the potential value of research discoveries. External financial reports, therefore, do not reflect such transactions.

2. Preparation of the statements requires estimation and judgment.

    To prepare the statements for the Corner Drugstore, *management* had to make estimates and judgments concerning:
    - How much of the cost of store equipment should be allocated as an expense of doing business for the year.
    - What unit costs should be used in determining the cost of the inventory, and what items of merchandise, if any, should be considered obsolete and eliminated from inventory.
    - What federal and state income tax expenses were incurred by the store on the year's operations.

    Conventional accounting statements are beguiling in their illusion of mathematical precision, as their preparation requires considerable estimation and judgment.

3. The statements are prepared on the assumption that the business will continue to operate indefinitely.

   Accordingly, because Corner Drugstore planned to use its store equipment rather than to sell it, the current market value of its store equipment is ignored in the company's external financial statements.

4. The accounting for assets is based upon acquisition cost rather than upon replacement cost.

   Store equipment is shown on the drugstore's balance sheet at cost of acquisition, less the portion of that cost previously allocated to expense. Inventory also is shown by the Corner Drugstore at acquistion cost, although inventory is sometimes reduced to current replacement cost for the sake of conservatism (see No. 5).

5. The statements are prepared conservatively.

   For example, inventories are shown on the balance sheet at the "lower of cost or market," where "market" is defined as "current replacement cost." This departure from the acquisition cost policy is deemed justified by the principle of conservatism. This principle holds: "Provide for all foreseeable losses, but do not recognize gain until it is realized by sale."

6. The statements ignore changes in the dollar's purchasing power.

   Corner Drugstore's investment in store equipment represented equipment acquired in different years with dollars of different purchasing power. At present, the accounting profession assumes that "dollars are dollars are dollars" and that they can be added together regardless of their vintage and their varying purchasing powers. When a portion of the "mixed vintage" investment in store equipment is allocated as depreciation expense of a given year, the depreciation expense is also expressed in dollars of mixed vintage and varying purchasing powers.

7. Companies may select from among several generally accepted accounting principles with respect to certain items contained in the financial statements.

   Although companies are required to apply their accounting principles on a consistent basis from year to year, different companies are free to choose different generally accepted accounting principles. Two common examples pertain to inventory valuation and depreciation. When making comparisons among companies, external users must understand the accounting principles upon which each company's financial statements were based. To do so requires users to read the "notes to the financial statements" carefully.

Corner Drugstore's financial statements have limitations. They are not as precise as they appear to be. The balance sheet does not express current market values. The owners' equity section of the balance sheet does not express the current market value of the owners' interests. The statement of income is expressed in more current dollars than is the balance sheet, but at least one of its expense deductions, depreciation, is expressed in dollars of mixed vintage. Many matters affecting the financial condition of the enterprise are not shown in the conventional accounting statements. Yet, despite their limitations, these statements are the accepted means for reporting to outsiders a corporation's financial activities and positions. Accordingly, their limitations must be fully recognized.

SUMMARY

Commencing in 1971, corporate external reports are required to include a statement of changes in financial position whenever financial statements purporting to present both financial position (balance sheet) and results of operations (statement of income and retained earnings) are issued. Although this newly required statement may be prepared to disclose either changes in cash or changes in working capital, most companies seem to choose the working capital approach. The major objective of the statement is to show what caused a change in a company's cash or in its working capital. As with the other required financial statements, the statement of changes in financial position has its limitations, and these limitations must be kept in mind when using the data contained therein.

5

Cash, Cash Equivalent, and Cash Flow

In this chapter we consider the accounting, reporting, and management of cash on hand, cash in bank, and cash temporarily invested in short-term debt securities. We explain the statement of cash receipts and disbursements and the cash flow statement—statements that can be used to summarize changes in cash for the past or to forecast them for the future. The chapter opens with a brief look at the relationship among cash, receivables, inventories, plant and equipment, and long-term investments.

The funds invested in a business by creditors and stockholders are invested by its management in five types of assets:

1. Cash and cash equivalent
2. Trade receivables
3. Inventories
4. Property, plant, and equipment
5. Long-term investments and other assets.

In a trading company, such as Corner Drugstore, daily transactions cause a continual shifting among cash, receivables, and inventory. In a manufacturing company, daily transactions cause a more complex pattern of changes among cash, receivables, inventories (in various stages of manufacture), and plant, property, and equipment.

CHANGES IN ASSETS: A TRADING COMPANY

For a trading company, the typical sequence of changes in assets is shown graphically in Illustration 5-1. Note these changes:

1. From cash to merchandise inventory when the company buys merchandise for sale.
2. From merchandise inventory to receivables when the company sells merchandise to customers on account.
3. From receivables to cash when the company collects customer accounts.

When Corner Drugstore (Chapter 3) purchased merchandise on account, a lapse of time occurred between the receipt of the merchandise and the outgo of cash to the suppliers. Ultimately, however, the change was from cash to merchandise. When the drugstore made sales for cash rather than on credit, the change was direct from merchandise to cash—rather than from merchandise to receivables to cash. The typical operating cycle, however, is from cash to merchandise to receivables and back to cash.

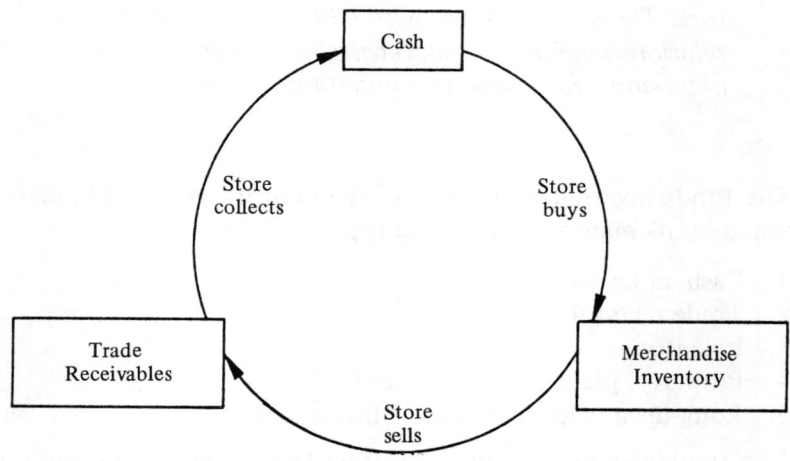

Illustration 5-1. Typical sequence of changes in assets for a trading company.

CHANGES IN ASSETS: A MANUFACTURING COMPANY

For a manufacturing company, goods to be sold are manufactured rather than purchased, and the typical sequence of changes among assets is much more complex than that for a trading company. Note, in Illustration 5-2, these changes:

1. From (a) cash to materials when the company buys materials (including purchased parts) and (b) materials to finished goods when the company uses materials to produce finished goods.
2. From cash to finished goods when the company pays for factory labor to convert materials into finished goods.
3. From cash to finished goods when the company pays for such factory costs as heat, light, power, building and equipment repairs, property taxes and insurance used in the conversion of materials into finished goods.
4. From (a) cash to property, plant, and equipment when the company acquires factory buildings, and (b) property, plant, and equipment to finished goods when the company periodically allocates part of its investment in factory buildings and equipment to the cost of producing finished goods.
5. From finished goods to receivables when the company sells finished goods to customers on account.
6. From receivables to cash when the company collects customer accounts.

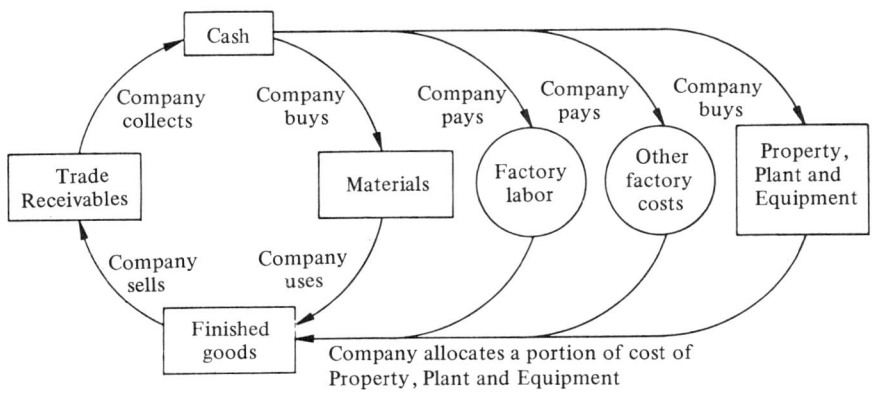

Illustration 5-2. Typical sequence of changes in assets for a manufacturing company.

A Note on Cost Accounting Practice

In the physical process of production, the usual progression is from materials to work-in-process to finished goods. In cost accounting, an account is usually set up for work-in-process. All factory costs of production are accumulated in this account before transfer to the finished goods account. In Illustration 5-2, we did not show work-in-process because for our present purposes it was simpler to omit it.

MANAGING CHANGES IN ASSETS

The job of management is to manage the changes in assets to accomplish the company's objectives. Management may set as the company's objectives:

1. To earn a satisfactory return on investment in assets.
2. To accommodate the business to seasonal, cyclical, growth, and random changes.
3. To aim for a pattern of investment in assets consistent with the sources of funds used to finance the business.
4. To assure continuity of the enterprise.
5. To assure continuity of management.

The relative weight given to each of these objectives will govern management in the patterns of asset investment it plans for the business. For example, if earning a satisfactory return on investment in assets is the controlling objective, managers will plan the minimum investment in each type of asset that will bring the highest rate of return. Our corner druggist will begin by asking himself why he should have more than a "zero" investment in cash, receivables, inventories, or equipment. He would maintain only the minimum cash required to operate the store. He would weigh any additional investment in receivables and inventories against the additional net income to be realized. For equipment, he would weigh the additional cost of short-term leasing against the additional investment required for acquisition by purchase.

If management needs to give more weight to accommodating the business to seasonal changes, the company may resort to seasonal borrowing for peak needs. Such borrowing may require that the company maintain "compensating" bank balances. Thus the source of financing would affect the pattern of asset investment. The more our corner druggist resorts to bank credit, the larger the related bank balance he will have to maintain.

If more weight is given to assuring continuity of present management or continuity of the enterprise, management may seek to finance the business more with equity capital than with debt. If, for example, our corner druggist wishes to forego borrowing from the bank, he will have to provide a buffer of cash to accommodate the store's operations to seasonal and cyclical fluctuations.

This brief discussion is illustrative rather than comprehensive. It is enough at this point for us to be aware of the effect of management objectives upon the pattern of asset investment and to be wary of looking for a standard pattern for all kinds of businesses.

CURRENT ASSETS, THE OPERATING CYCLE, AND THE CURRENT RATIO

In the glossary at the end of this book, we define *current assets* as cash and other assets that normally will be converted into cash or utilized within a year (or within the operating cycle of the particular business entity if this is longer than a year). We can now define the *operating cycle* as the average time period between the purchase of merchandise (or materials) and the collection of cash from customers after the merchandise (or manufactured product) has been sold. The operating cycle is indicated graphically in Illustrations 5-1 and 5-2. The *current ratio* is a comparison between the company's investment in current assets and the funds supplied by short-term creditors, shown as current liabilities. In Illustration 4-1, the Corner Drugstore at March 31, 1979, had current assets of $19,400 and current liabilities of $8,500, so its current ratio was $19,400 to $8,500, or 2.3 to 1; at March 31, 1980, the ratio was $25,975 to $10,500, or 2.5 to 1.

THE NATURE OF CASH AND CASH EQUIVALENT

Cash and cash equivalent consist of cash on hand, cash in bank, and marketable securities representing a temporary investment of cash.

Cash on hand may be in the form of special cash funds for operating purposes, such as change funds maintained by retail stores, or cash collections (currency, coins, and checks), received from customers and others, on hand awaiting deposit in bank.

Cash in bank represents the balances on deposit with banks. The bank may not record deposit and check transactions on the same date that the company records them. Thus, the balance shown by the company's books usually differs from that shown by the bank's, although the two are reconcilable. On the company's balance sheet, cash in bank is stated at the balance shown on the company's books, not the bank's.

Marketable securities, representing a temporary investment of cash, are usually in the form of readily salable short-maturity fixed obligations on which the company earns interest.

CASH MANAGEMENT AND COMPENSATING BALANCES

The company maintains its investment in cash in bank for one or more of the following reasons:

1. To cover the amount of customer checks in process of collection.
2. To provide a margin or "safety-valve" against possible errors in cash forecasting.
3. To assure freedom from the necessity of borrowing from the bank.
4. To meet the bank's requirement for a *compensating balance* (a) against the bank's loan(s) or line of credit extended to the business and (b) to "pay" the bank for servicing the checking account and for other bank services.

Let's discuss each of these reasons.

The company maintains a balance at least equal to the amount of customer checks in process of collection. When our corner drugstore deposited its customers' checks in the bank, the bank undertook to collect them through the check collection facilities of the banking system. The period needed to collect checks deposited varies according to the location of the banks upon which they are drawn. Customer checks drawn on the bank in which they are deposited are "collected" the same day that they are deposited, those drawn on other local banks may be collected the day following deposit; while those drawn on out-of-town banks may take two, three, or even four days to collect.

Despite the lag in collecting deposited checks, normal banking practice is to credit the depositor's account in full the day that the checks are deposited. In the case of Corner Drugstore and its bank, neither the store's nor the bank's books showed that a part of the store's recorded balance represented checks in the process of collection. But both the store and the bank operated on the basis that the recorded balance would be sufficient to cover the amount of customer checks in process of collection.

The bank balance is maintained to provide against errors in cash forecasting. Ideally, if the Corner Drugstore could forecast its cash receipts and disbursements exactly, it could keep its investment in cash in bank to a minimum. The less precisely it can forecast, the larger the safety valve or buffer it must maintain in the form of cash in bank.

The company may maintain a bank balance sufficient to avoid borrowing from the bank. The objective of some companies may be to "keep out of the bank," that is, to avoid borrowing from the bank. To avoid borrowing, these companies must have cash in excess of needs in periods of seasonal and cyclical slack. When a company uses its cash balance as a buffer for seasonal and cyclical fluctuations, its return on investment in assets is usually lower than if it borrowed for peak needs. Companies may, however, have valid reasons for maintaining buffer cash balances and for refusing to borrow, despite the lowered return on investment.

The bank balance is maintained (a) to meet the bank's requirements for a compensating balance against loans or line of credit, and (b) to cover cost of bank services. When a company opens a bank account, the bank will usually acquaint the company's officers with the bank's requirements for a compensating balance sufficiently large to meet the compensating balance requirement against loan(s) or line of credit extended and to cover the cost of bank services.

When a company negotiates an agreement with its bank for a *line of credit*—the bank's agreement to lend the company funds up to an agreed amount during, say, the next calendar year—the bank may require that the company maintain a *collected balance* of 10 percent of the line of credit, or 20 percent of the loans actually made. From time to time, the bank will calculate the *collected balance* of each business customer in the following manner:

Average daily book balance for the month............ (This balance is computed by adding together the balance for each day in the month as shown on the bank's account for the customer and by dividing the total by the number of days in the month.)	$10,000
Deducting average daily "float" for the month........... (The bank determines for each check deposited the number of days required to collect the check, multiplies dollars by days, sums for the month, and then divides by number of days in the month.)	(400)
Average daily collected balance for the month...........	$ 9,600

Disclosure of compensating balance requirements is required by the Securities and Exchange Commission. Dan River, Inc., made the following disclosure in its annual report for 1978:

> Compensating Balances—Informal lines of credit agreements with several banks require the company to maintain average cash compensating balances principally equal to 20 percent of the average outstanding short-term bank loans or 10 percent of the amount of the credit line, whichever is higher.... In 1978 the average compensating balance required to be maintained amounted to $4,354,000 and the amount required at December 30, 1978 was $4,008,000 after adjustment for estimated average float.

CASH IN BANK: CHECKS AND DEPOSITS

Conventional accounting for cash in bank is not complex. Deposits are recorded as increases, checks as decreases, in the Cash in Bank account.

The time for accounting recognition of a check is the date the company issues the check. This brings the check immediately under accounting control. If the company draws a check to an out-of-town supplier on August 27, the check is recorded as of that date, even though several days may elapse before the check gets to, and is paid by, the company's bank. When a company issues a check in payment of a bill to an out-of-town supplier, time elapses (1) in the transmission of the check to the supplier, (2) in the supplier's recording and depositing the check, and (3) in the transmission of the check through the banking system from the supplier's bank to the company's bank. A study by one company indicated that the average time lapse between the dates checks were drawn and the dates they were ultimately paid by the company's bank was eight days for checks drawn to out-of-town suppliers and three days for checks drawn to employees (for weekly wages).

The time lags that exist between the company's records and the bank's records explain why the daily balances shown in the company's cash in bank account may differ considerably from the "average collected balance" used by the bank in its analysis of the company's account for service charges and for compensating balance requirements against borrowings. Furthermore, whenever the company receives a bank statement, usually at a month-end, it should prove its accounting record of cash in bank with the bank's record by preparing a reconciliation of the bank account.

Bank Reconciliation

To prepare a reconciliation of the bank account as of the month-end, the company compares the checks it receives from the bank against its check disbursement record and prepares a list of outstanding checks. It then compares the deposits shown on the bank statement with those in the company's records, and notes any deposits not on the bank statement, or vice versa. Notes are made of any special bank "Debit Memos" or "Credit Memos" that have not been recorded by the company. One form of bank reconciliation, Illustration 5-3, is in two parts. The first begins with the month-end balance shown by the bank statement and works to an *adjusted balance*. The second part begins with the month-end balance shown by the cash in bank account in the company's ledger and works to an adjusted balance. The adjusted balance should be the same in both parts.

Note, in Illustration 5-3, that the second part of the reconciliation provides the data for entries to be made for any bank Debit Memos or Credit Memos not previously recorded by the company, and for correction of any company errors discovered in the reconciliation. The second part of Illustration 5-3 shows the following entries to be in order:

Cash in Bank (A)	Incr 234.00		
Notes Receivable (A)		Decr	225.00
Accounts Payable (L)		Incr	9.00
Trade Receivables (A)	Incr 63.27		
Cash in Bank (A)		Decr	63.27

CASH AND CASH EQUIVALENT ON THE BALANCE SHEET

Balance sheet treatment of cash and cash equivalent raises two questions. First, at what value should the items comprising cash and

---

Illustration 5-3

Two-Part Form for Reconciliation of Bank Account

Bank's Records

Balance at month-end, per bank statement		$3,481.93
Add:		
Deposits in transit at month-end (per list)	$688.05	
Bank error in charging our account with check drawn by another company	85.00	773.05
		$4,254.98
Deduct:		
Checks outstanding at month-end (per list)		1,882.70
Adjusted Balance at month-end		$2,372.28

Our Records

Balance at month-end, per our records	$2,201.55
Add:	
Bank Credit Memo for collection of customer note not yet recorded by us	225.00
Error on our check #1465 drawn for $123.00 but recorded by us as $132.00	9.00
	$2,435.55
Deduct:	
Bank Debit Memo for check of our customer, J. A. Best, returned for "Insufficient Funds," not yet entered on our records	63.27
Adjusted Balance at month-end	$2,372.28

cash equivalent be shown? Second, under what classification should the items be shown?

Valuation

Cash on hand and cash in bank are shown at realizable value. For cash on hand, the realizable value is the amount of the change fund, petty cash fund, cash on hand awaiting deposit, etc. For cash in bank, realizable value is the amount of the adjusted balance shown on the reconciliation of the bank account at the balance sheet date.

Marketable securities representing a temporary investment of cash in the form of readily salable short-maturity debt instruments are carried at cost if cost is less than market value at the balance sheet date. (In such cases, market value may be disclosed parenthetically.) When market value is substantially less than cost, this difference should be disclosed, and in such case the securities should be shown at market. If cost is slightly less than market, the securities may continue to be shown at cost with disclosure of the market value.

Classification

Cash on hand and cash in bank available for current operations are usually shown simply as Cash in the current asset section of the balance sheet. Cash not available for current operations is not shown in the current asset section.

The *Restatement and Revision of Accounting Research Bulletins*, issued in 1953 by the American Institute of Certified Public Accountants (Chapter 1), discusses the nature of current assets and indicates that there should be *excluded* from current assets "cash and claims to cash which are restricted as to withdrawal or use for other than current operation, are designated for expenditure in the acquisition or construction of noncurrent assets, or are segregated for the liquidation of long-term debts." Such assets should be shown elsewhere on the balance sheet.

Cash advances to suppliers and others, and cash deposits for specific purposes (insurance, public utilities, etc.) are not shown as Cash. Such advances and deposits are classified sometimes as current assets, sometimes as noncurrent.

Marketable securities in the form of short-term fixed obligations and representing an investment of temporarily unneeded cash are sometimes combined with cash and shown as Cash and Cash Equivalent under current assets. Normally, marketable equity securities are not considered as cash equivalent. In those cases when marketable equity securities are included in current assets, FASB statement No. 12 requires (1) that they be carried at the lower of aggregate cost or market value and (2) that the aggregate cost and aggregate market value be disclosed.

Marketable securities, either equity or fixed-obligation, bought for purposes other than temporary investment of unneeded cash, are generally shown under long-term investments in the noncurrent section of the balance sheet.

STATEMENT OF CASH RECEIPTS AND DISBURSEMENTS

At the end of an accounting period a statement of cash receipts and disbursements can be prepared. This statement is based upon a summary of the transactions recorded in the cash account in the company's ledger.

A summary of the Corner Drugstore's cash account for the fiscal year 1979 is reproduced in Illustration 5-4.

Illustration 5-4

Corner Drugstore's Ledger Account for Cash for Fiscal 1979
(Source: Illustration 3-4)

Cash (A)

4-1-78 Balance		-0-	(E)	Pd. for store eq.	10,000
(A)	From capital stock	10,000	(H)	Cash sales returned	500
(D)	Bank loan payable	9,000	(J)	Pd. mdse. suppliers	53,600
(F)	Cash sales	30,300	(K)	Paid rent	3,600
(I)	Collections of receiv.	40,500	(L)	Paid employees	14,600
			(M)	Paid for utilities	450
			(N)	Pd. est. income tax	600
			(O)	Pd. other expenses	500
			(P)	Pd. on bank loan—On principal $1,500, Interest $450	1,950
			(S)	Paid dividends	1,500
				3-31-79 To balance	2,500
		89,800			89,800
3-31-79 Balance		2,500			

A simple form of cash receipts and disbursements for the drugstore would show:

Cash balance at beginning of fiscal year (4/1/78)	$	0
Add: Cash receipts during the year (In order summarized in Illustration 5-4.)		89,800
		89,800
Deduct: Cash disbursements during the year (In order summaraized in Illustration 5-4.)		87,300
Cash balance at the end of fiscal year (3/31/79)	$	2,500

In Illustration 5-5, we have presented the same information in a more orderly format.

The format used in Illustration 5-5 permits a ready conversion to a "cash flow statement" that shows:

1. "Cash internally generated" from transactions associated with purchasing, selling, and collecting.

Illustration 5-5

Corner Drugstore, Inc.
Statement of Cash Receipts and Disbursements
For the Year Ended March 31, 1979

Cash Receipts:		
Cash sales (less $500 paid for cash sales returned)		$29,800
Collections on customer accounts.		40,500
Cash received from customers.		70,300
Proceeds from issue of capital stock		10,000
Borrowing from bank.		9,000
Total Cash Receipts.		89,300
Less Cash Disbursements:		
For payments on supplier accounts.	$53,600	
For payments to employees	14,600	
For rent, utilities and other expenses.	4,550	
For payments of interest on bank loan.	450	
For payments on estimated income taxes	600	
Sub-total.	73,800	
For acquisition of store equipment	10,000	
For dividends to stockholders.	1,500	
For reduction in principal of bank loan	1,500	
Total Cash Disbursements		86,800
Net increase in cash account in fiscal 1979		2,500
Add: Cash balance, April 1, 1978.		-0-
Cash balance, March 31, 1979.		$ 2,500

2. Cash outflow for

> Acquisition of property, plant, and equipment (in excess of any dispositions).
> Dividends to stockholders.

3. Financing and other cash inflows and outflows.

Converting Illustration 5-5, we arrive at the following "cash flow" summary for the Corner Drugstore:

1. Cash received from customers, *$70,300*, was less than cash paid out to suppliers and employees and cash paid for store expenses, interest, and income tax, (*$73,800*).
   Thus "cash internally generated" was a *minus*.......... ($ 3,500)

2. Payments for acquisition of store equipment, (*$10,000*), and for dividends to stockholders, (*$1,500*), amounted to............................... (11,500)

3. Cash received from financing transactions:
   From issue of capital stock $10,000
   From net increase in bank loan   7,500
   A total of.   17,500

So the increase the store's cash balance from *zero* at 4/1/78 to *$2,500* at 3/31/79 was .... $ 2,500

(Note that for the purposes of the above summary we have shown uses of cash enclosed in parentheses, sources without parentheses.)

The cash receipts and disbursements statement is prepared for internal use only, primarily for cash management and cash forecasting. The *form* of the statement serves as one model for cash forecasting. Cash forecasting begins with a forecast of sales, from which forecasts of cash sales and collections on account can be made. The forecast of sales volume aids in forecasting cash outlays for operating expenses and income tax payments. All these items combined go to make up what we have termed "cash internally generated." There then remain the tasks of forecasting cash dividends to stockholders, cash outlays for property, plant, and equipment, cash receipts from borrowing and issue of capital stock, and cash payments on debt principal.

CASH FLOW STATEMENT

A cash flow statement, developed from a published statement of changes in financial position, can give substantially the same information as the statement of cash receipts and disbursements prepared for internal use from the cash account in the ledger.

As indicated in Chapter 4, the statement of changes in financial position "may be prepared so as to disclose either changes in working capital or changes in cash." If the statement uses the working capital format, our first task is to analyze the schedule of working capital changes to determine, within this schedule, which items represent Uses of cash and which represent Sources of cash, according to the following scheme:

Uses	Sources
Increase in a current asset	Decrease in a current asset
Decrease in a current liability	Increase in a current liability

Apply this analysis to the statement of changes in financial position for Corner Drugstore for fiscal 1979, shown in Illustration 4-5.

From Illustration 4-5

	1979 Working Capital Incr. or (Decr.)	Use or Source	Why Use or Source
Current Assets:			
Cash	$ 2,500	Use	Incr. in current asset
Trade receivables	4,200	Use	Incr. in current asset
Merchandise inventory	12,700	Use	Incr. in current asset
Current Liabilities:			
Accounts, wages, and utilities payable	(4,700)	Source	Incr. in current liab.
Income tax payable	(2,300)	Source	Incr. in current liab.
Bank loan (current)	(1,500)	Source	Incr. in current liab.
Increase in Working Capital	$10,900		

The next step, in converting the published statement of changes in financial position to the cash flow statement format is to group the various Sources and Uses into four categories:

1. Net Income Adjusted (NIA)—that is, net income (after income tax) before deduction of noncash expenses and before addition of noncash revenue.

    In Illustration 4-5, the NIA figure is $6,400 — net income, $5,400, plus noncash expense for depreciation, $1,000.
2. Changes in receivables, inventories, payables and accruals, and income tax liability (RIPT) which changes act as adjustments of Net Income Adjusted to give "cash internally generated."

    In Illustration 4-5, these items are found in the schedule of working capital changes:

Increase in receivables	(4,200) a Use
Increase in merchandise inventory	(12,700) a Use
Increase in accounts, wage, and utilities payable	4,700 a Source
Increase in income tax payable	2,300 a Source
A net adjustment of	(9,900) a Use

3. Discretionary Outgoes (D. O.)—for acquisitions of property, plant, and equipment (in excess of dispositions), and for cash dividends to stockholders.

    In Illustration 4-5, these items are:

Acquisition of store equipment	(10,000) a Use
Payment of dividends	(1,500) a Use
A total of	(11,500) a Use

4. Financing and Other (F. & O.)—for financing and all other changes (except the change in Cash itself).

    In Illustration 4-5, these items are:

Issuance of capital stock	10,000 a Source
Net increase in bank loan in fiscal 1979	7,500 a Source

This information, taken from the statement of changes in financial position (Illustration 4-5), can now be brought together in a cash flow statement. Note that this form carries the instruction that "changes that decrease cash are shown in parentheses," so we will show *Uses* in parentheses and *Sources* without.

Ideally we should "checkoff" with a check mark, each item on the statement of changes in financial position as we use it in preparing the cash flow statement to make sure that we leave out no item

Cash, Cash Equivalent, and Cash Flow 81

and that the statement will prove, at the bottom, with the change in Cash.

The Cash Flow Statement for the Corner Drugstore, Inc., for its fiscal year ended March 31, 1979, is shown as Illustration 5-6. Trace each item shown in the previous discussion of the four categories to its entry on the cash flow statement.

Note that Illustration 5-6 agrees, in summary, with the statement of cash receipts and disbursements (Illustration 5-5), with respect to

Cash internally generated	($ 3,500)
Discretionary outgoes	(11,500)
Financing and other	17,500
Increase in cash	$ 2,500

CASH FLOW STATEMENTS DERIVED FROM COMPANY ANNUAL REPORTS

It is useful in interpreting published statements of changes in financial position to convert such statements to a cash flow statement by using the form in Illustration 5-6.

The following discussion considers in more detail the four categories of changes which affect cash and cash equivalent.

1. *Net income (after tax) before deduction of noncash expenses and before addition of noncash revenue.*

Until recent years, the most common adjustment to net income after tax was the addition of depreciation as a source. Depreciation is deducted as an expense in determining net income, but depreciation does not involve a cash outlay. (The cash outlay involved is, of course, the capital expenditure which went for acquiring the assets being depreciated.) The addition of depreciation here simply reverses the earlier deduction—to convert the net income figure into a cash income figure.

Other kinds of noncash expenses and revenues have appeared in recent years to make the translation of reported net income to cash net income more complex. Some of these other adjustments are:

Deferred income taxes. This tax expense is reported on the income statement but does not involve a cash outlay. The amount of

Illustration 5-6

CASH FLOW STATEMENT
(Changes that decrease cash are shown in parentheses)

Company Corner Drugstore, Inc. in _____ of Dollars	Year Sales	1979 74,500		
I. Net Income		5,400		
Add: Depreciation		1,000		
Add: Other noncash expenses				
Subtract: Noncash revenues				
Net income before depreciation and other noncash expenses and revenues		6,400		
II. This could have represented cash inflow but it did not happen this way because the company:				
A. Collected (less than) more than it billed customers, as shown in *Receivables* (incr.) decrease		(4,200)		
B. Bought and mfd. (more than) less than the cost of goods shipped, as shown in *Inventories* (incr.) decrease		(12,700)		
C. Paid out (more than) less than the costs it incurred, as shown in *Payables & Accruels* (decr.) increase		4,700		
D. Paid out (more than) less than income tax incurred as shown in *Income Tax Liabilities* (decr.) increase		2,300		
Total four items:		(9,900)		
so that "cash internally generated" was		(3,500)		
III. There were "discretionary" outgoes of cash for:				
Acquisitions of property, plant and equipment (in excess of dispositions)		(10,000)		
Dividends to stockholders		(1,500)		
Total discretionary outgoes		(11,500)		
Cash internally generated less discretionary outgoes		(15,000)		
IV. Financing and other cash inflows and outgoes were:				
Issue of Capital Stock		10,000		
Net Increase in Bank Loan Payable		7,500		
Total financing and other flows		17,500		
With the effect on the company's cash (and cash equivalent) being an increase (decr.) of		2,500		

Cash, Cash Equivalent, and Cash Flow   83

this expense each year becomes an addition to deferred income tax liability on the balance sheet.

Equity in profits in nonconsolidated affiliated or subsidiary companies. This equity occurs when the parent company takes its share of the affiliated or subsidiary company's profit into its income statement. This, then, is noncash revenue, and so for computing cash net income, the transaction must be reversed. If dividends are received from affiliated or subsidiary companies, they show up later under the Financing and Other category. (This is known as the *equity method* of accounting for affiliates and unconsolidated subsidiaries.)

2. *Changes in receivables, inventories, payables and accruals, and income tax liability* (the current liability, not deferred tax liability) are in effect uses and sources of cash that are closely tied to operating policies, practices and results.

3. *Discretionary outgoes*, capital expenditures and dividends, are two major uses of cash that are not a part of current operations. These outgoes are authorized not by the company's operating management, but by the board of directors.

4. *Financing and Other* is a group of cash sources and uses that shows the major financing flows and other flows not shown elsewhere. The short-term portion of long-term debt is combined with the long-term portion to show the flows that result from total change in long-term debt.

Let us derive cash flow statements for Caterpillar Tractor Co. for 1978 and 1979, based upon its statement of changes in financial position, Statement 3, 1979 Annual Report (reproduced in Chapter 6).

1. Since Caterpillar uses the net current assets (working capital) format, we go to the schedule of net current asset changes and indicate by (U) or S whether each change represents a Use or Source according to the following scheme:

Use	Source
Increase in a current asset	Decrease in a current asset
Decrease in a current liability	Increase in a current liability

Then we indicate for each item whether it is RIPT, DO, or F&O. In Illustration 5-7, we show the designations (U), S, RIPT, and F&O for Caterpillar's schedule of net current asset changes.

2. Now we go to the top of Caterpillar's Statement 3 and indicate whether the change should be included as NIA, RIPT, DO, or F&O. We also show whether each change is (U) or S. See Illustration 5-8.

3. Using our annotated version of Caterpillar's statement of changes in financial position, Illustrations 5-7 and 5-8, we enter the figures appropriately on the cash flow statement. As we enter each figure, we check it off on the statement of changes in financial position. The completed cash flow statement form is shown as Illustration 5-9. Trace the figures on Illustration 5-9 from Illustrations 5-7 and 5-8.

LEARNING FROM THE CASH FLOW STATEMENT

The form should help you to grasp the significant factors in the way a company has managed its cash flows in the changing economic environment from year to year. It should help you also to reconcile a

Illustration 5-7
Analysis of Schedule of Net Current Assets (Working Capital) Changes of Caterpillar Tractor Co. for 1979 and 1978
(In millions of dollars)

		1979		1978	
Cash and short-term investments	Cash	(97.3)	S	35.1	(U)
Receivable from customers and others	RIPT	(75.1)	S	119.7	(U)
Prepaid expenses, etc.	F&O	3.1	(U)	(12.5)	S
Inventories	RIPT	147.9	(U)	233.7	(U)
Net change in current assets		(21.4)		376.0	
Notes payable	F&O	291.6	S	25.3	S
Payable to material suppliers and others	RIPT	(64.0)	(U)	175.8	S
Taxes based on income	RIPT	(103.3)	(U)	58.5	S
Long-term debt due within one year	F&O	24.7	S	21.7	S
Net change in current liabilities		149.0		281.3	
Increase (or decrease) in net current assets during year		(170.4)		94.7	

Illustration 5-8

Analysis of Top Part of Caterpillar Tractor Co.'s Changes in Consolidated Financial Position
(In millions of dollars)

		1979		1978	
Additions to net current assets:					
Operations:					
Profit for year.	NIA	$491.6		$566.3	
Items affecting profit for the year, but not affecting net current assets:					
Depreciation.	NIA	311.8		257.1	
Deferred taxes based on income. . .	NIA	(47.4)		(12.1)	
Equity in profit of affiliated companies.	NIA	(30.2)		.8	
Profit of subsidiary credit companies.	NIA	(3.5)		(1.1)	
Net current assets provided from operations	NIA	722.3	S	811.0	S
Long-term debt	F&O	2.8	S	91.4	S
Capital assets sold or scrapped.	DO	4.2	S	2.8	S
Common stock sold for cash under stock options.	F&O	3.1	S	4.5	S
Common stock issued upon conversion of convertible debentures	F&O	–		.3	S
Dividends from affiliated companies	F&O	6.0	S	7.1	S
Dividends from subsidiary credit companies	F&O	1.0	S	–	
Reduction in advances to subsidiary credit companies	F&O	–		8.7	S
Reclassification of other assets	F&O	10.8	S	–	
Other.	F&O	5.7	S	(4.7)	(U)
		755.9		921.1	
Reduction of net current assets for:					
Cash dividends.	DO	181.5	(U)	161.8	(U)
Land, buildings, machinery, and equip . . .	DO	675.9	(U)	543.4	(U)
Long-term debt	F&O	68.9	(U)	84.4	(U)
Reclassification of receivables	F&O	–		36.8	(U)
		926.3		826.4	
Increase (or decrease) in net current assets during year		(170.4)		94.7	
Net current assets at beginning of year		1,391.2		1,296.5	
Net current assets at end of year		$1,220.8		$1,391.2	

company's reported net income with the change in its cash balance. Several interesting analyses can be made:

1. The percentage change of the four RIPT items can be compared to changes in sales and net income. One would expect receiv-

Illustration 5-9

CASH FLOW STATEMENT
(Changes that decrease cash are shown in parentheses)

Company Caterpillar Tractor Co.
in millions of Dollars

	Year	1979	1978
	Sales	7,613.2	7,219.2
I. Net Income		491.6	566.3
Add: Depreciation		311.8	257.1
Add: Other noncash expenses – Deferred inc. tax		(47.4)	(12.1)
Subtract: Noncash revenues – Equity in Pft. subs. & Affil.		(33.7)	(.3)
Net income before depreciation and other noncash expenses and revenues		722.3	811.0
II. And this could have represented cash inflow but it did not happen this way because the company			
A. Collected (less than) more than it billed customers, as shown in *Receivables* (increase) decrease		75.1	(119.7)
B. Bought and mfd. (more than) less than the cost of goods shipped, as shown in *Inventories* (increase) decrease		(147.9)	(233.7)
C. Paid out (more than) less than the costs it incurred, as shown in *Payables & Accruals* (decrease) increase		(64.0)	175.8
D. Paid out (more than) less than income tax incurred, as shown in *Income Tax Liabilities* (decrease) increase		(103.3)	58.5
Total Four Items		(240.1)	(119.1)
so that "cash internally generated" was		482.2	691.9
III. There were "discretionary" outgoes of cash for: Acquisitions of property, plant & equipment (in excess of dispositions)		(671.7)	(540.6)
Dividends to stockholders		(181.5)	(161.8)
Total Discretionary Outgoes		(853.2)	(702.4)
Cash internally generated less discretionary outgoes		(371.0)	(10.5)
IV. Financing & other cash inflows & outgoes were: Net increase (decrease) in L-T debt (<&> 1 yr.)		(41.4)	28.7
Increase in S-T notes payable		291.6	25.3
Common Stock issued		3.1	4.8
Dividends & advances to/from affil. & sub. co.		7.0	15.8
Reclassification of receivables		–	(36.8)
Other (1979–16.5-3.1) (1978–12.5-4.7)		13.4	7.8
Total Financing and Other Flows		273.7	45.6
With the effect on the company's cash (and cash equivalent) being an increase (decrease) of		(97.3)	35.1

ables, inventory, and payables to fluctuate with sales, and tax liabilities to follow net income. Analysis of these four items should indicate whether variations are as expected or out of line, and if the latter, what the likely reasons may be.
2. A comparison of Cash Internally Generated with Discretionary Outgoes shows the extent to which the company was able to pay dividends and cover capital expenditures from internal sources.
3. The Financing and Other category shows how the firm is covering a cash deficit (or disposing of a cash surplus) resulting from cash internally generated less discretionary outgoes. One can check whether long-term sources are being matched with long-term needs, whether debt or equity is being used, and whether there are any other major sources or uses of cash.
4. One can also use this format for cash forecasting by filling in expected changes for the coming year. When the projections called for by the cash flow form have been made, one can see the major outlines of the projected cash flow pattern for the firm. By putting all this information on one page, one can discern the important interdependence of the several parts of the cash flow process.

FRAUD AND INTERNAL CONTROL

One of management's responsibilities is to safeguard the assets of the business against fraud by employees and others. Because cash and marketable securities are easily negotiated, safeguarding these assets is more difficult than safeguarding other kinds of assets.

Internal control is the principal means of safeguarding cash and marketable securities. By the term *internal control* we mean an allocation of duties among employees so that no one employee has complete responsibility for handling and recording a transaction from initiation to completion, the work of one employee checks against the work of another, and the subdivision of duties affords an automatic internal control over cash, securities, and other assets.

For example, in handling and recording of checks received from customers through the mail,

- One employee may receive the mail, open it, list the checks received, and arrive at the total, say $736.05.
- Another employee may prepare the deposit but, before taking

it to the bank, he will check the total of $736.05 against the total determined by the first employee.
- A third employee may record the amount received from each customer on the customer's account in the subsidiary ledger, and prove the total of the day's entries with the summary total of $736.05.

At times, management may find that internal control procedures conflict with other operating considerations. This conflict occurs most frequently in the area of customer relations. For example, in handling a cash sale, it might be good internal control for the sales clerk to send the cash to the cashier; yet, for good customer service, it might be better for the sales clerk to handle the whole transaction.

The job of management is to arrange an internal control that does not unduly interfere with the major operating activities of buying, manufacturing, selling, and collecting. Some years ago, Sir Simon Marks of England's Marks & Spencer stores resolved the dilemma for his organization by cutting out much of the internal paperwork, thus providing better customer service at lower cost. At the other extreme are instances where the discovery of employee fraud may bring about cumbersome internal control procedures which markedly affect customer relations. Balancing good relations with customers and adequate internal control among employees can be difficult.

Computer-based accounting and information systems have changed the nature of internal control. They have not changed the potential for fraud or the need for internal procedures to forestall it.

SUMMARY

Conventional accounting for cash and cash equivalent is not complex, although some problems are encountered in accounting for Cash in Bank. Both the company and the bank record deposits when the deposits are made, despite the fact that there may be a lag of several days before customer checks are collected by the bank. The time for accounting recognition of a check disbursement is the date the check is drawn. The bank records a check when it pays the check, and this may be a number of days after the business records the check. This lag introduces a continuing difference between the records of the company and the records of the bank, as indicated by the amount of outstanding checks in the reconciliation of the bank account.

In the management of bank balances, supplementary information to that afforded by the usual accounting records may be required. For example, a company may determine the time lag between the date it draws checks to its larger suppliers and the date these checks are paid by the bank, and take this time lag into account in managing the company's bank account. The reason that conventional accounting provides for the recording of checks when they are issued is to bring them under accounting control immediately as a matter of internal control. This, nevertheless, creates a gap between the data afforded by conventional accounting and the data needed by management to manage the company's bank balances.

In managing the changing mix of its investment in assets, management has the problem of determining how much investment in cash and cash equivalent it should maintain. This will be governed in part by how the business is financed, how much it is subjected to seasonal and cyclical swings, how much it desires to "stay out of the bank," and how well it can forecast its cash changes. In managing the company's bank balances, management needs to know (1) how the banks administer their requirements for compensating balances against loans and lines of credit, (2) what service charges the banks make, and (3) how much the company must rely upon its banks as a source of financing. There may be a conflict between strict return on investment considerations on the part of business management and the desire for substantial customer deposit balances on the part of bank management.

The cash receipts and disbursements statement is prepared for internal use only, primarily for cash management and cash forecasting. The form of the statement can be designed to show cash internally generated, discretionary outgoes for capital expenditures and dividends, and financing and other flows. A cash flow statement embodying this same information can be developed from a company's published statement of changes in financial position. The cash flow statement can help the user understand

- how a company has managed its cash flows,
- how changes in receivables, inventories, payables and accruals, and income tax liability have affected cash internally generated,
- the extent to which cash internally generated has covered discretionary outgoes for dividends and capital expenditures.
- the extent to which external financing via debt and equity has been used, and
- how all this ties into the change in the company's cash balance.

The format for the cash flow statement serves as a convenient model for cash forecasting.

The responsibility of management to safeguard assets is especially acute in the matter of cash and cash equivalent. Internal control is a main defense against employee fraud. But a proper balance needs to be struck between the requirements of internal control and the way in which the business performs its primary functions of buying, manufacturing, selling, and collecting.

6

Annual Reports to Stockholders

This chapter has two purposes: to illustrate and explain published financial statements, and to discuss a few of the contemporary controversies in external reporting.

The three major financial statements we will discuss are the statement of income and retained earnings (sometimes referred to as the statement of operations), the balance sheet or statement of financial position, and the statement of changes in financial position.

To illustrate the three types of statements, we present selected financial statements and related footnotes from the 1979 Annual Report of Caterpillar Tractor Company. The general nature of each statement will be described with particular attention given to the effects that the basic concepts discussed in Chapter 1 have on the way the statement is presented. Caterpillar Tractor is used because its annual report is more comprehensive than many. The format of some of the statements and the nomenclature used are somewhat different from those used thus far but will give us an opportunity to see a "real world" report.

STATEMENT OF INCOME AND RETAINED EARNINGS

The statement of income shows for one accounting period, the change in owners' equity arising from the sale of products and service to customers, less the cost of products and services sold and less other expenses of the period. Accordingly, the statement of income shows sales, expenses, and net income *for a period of time*.

1. *Sales.* Sales represents the collectible total, in dollars, for which customers were billed for sales of products and services during the period (without regard to whether the company has yet collected for the sales).
2. *Expenses.* Expenses are the total costs, in dollars, that are incurred in connection with and are properly matched against the sales made during the period. Expenses include:
   a. cost of goods sold;
   b. selling, general, and administrative expenses;
   c. interest on money borrowed; and
   d. income taxes.
3. *Net Income for the Period.* Net income is determined by deducting expenses from sales, and then adding Other Revenue (if any). Net income is the amount, in dollars, which has been earned for the corporation's stockholders during the period in accordance with generally accepted accounting principles.

The statement of retained earnings shows for a period of time:

> Retained Earnings at the beginning of the period.
> Plus: Net Income for the period.
> Less: Dividends declared this period.
> Retained Earnings at the end of the period.

The statement of retained earnings may be combined into one statement with the statement of income, the combined statement called *the statement of income and retained earnings*. Caterpillar Tractor Company presents a combined statement of income and retained earnings to which it gives the title "Consolidated Results of Operations," reproduced as Statement 1 on page 94.

Let us look at Statement 1, Caterpillar's comparative statements of income and retained earnings for the years 1979 and 1978. Note the following characteristics:

1. The word "consolidated" in the statement title, "Consolidated Results of Operations," is explained by the company in Note 1A as follows:

> Caterpillar Tractor Company has investments in subsidiaries, all of which are wholly owned, and in two affiliated companies, which are 50% owned. The accompanying financial statements include the accounts of Caterpillar Tractor Company and all of its subsidiaries except its two credit subsidiaries.

Business entity was the first basic concept listed in Chapter 1, and it was there noted that when ". . . one corporation owns all or most of the capital stock of other corporations, and this group of corporations is operated as a single economic unit, the external financial reports may be 'consolidated' for the group and the business entity is then identified as the *consolidated group of corporations*."

2. The statement is expressed "in millions of dollars," shown to one decimal place. Caterpillar is unique in rounding to this extent, though an increasing number of companies are showing their statements in thousands of dollars. Caterpillar's rounding of figures to tenths of millions indicates that the figures are approximations. Thus, the company has recognized the basic concepts of *materiality* and *use of estimates and exercise of judgment*.

3. Statement 1 shows for the year 1979:

Sales	$7,613.2 million
Costs allocated to year	7,155.3 million
	457.9 million
Equity in affiliated companies and subsidiary credit companies	33.7 million
Profit for year—consolidated	$ 491.6 million

Profit per share of common stock (1979):
   assuming no dilution $5.69
   assuming full dilution $5.50

The $5.69 figure of profit per share for 1979 was obtained by dividing the $491.6 million profit for the year by the weighted average number of the company's stock outstanding. Profit per share assuming full dilution gives effect to the potential conversion of the 5.5% Convertible Subordinated Debenture and unexercised stock options. (See Note 6 on page 100.) To a stockholder, *earnings per share* is the

Statement 1: Caterpillar Tractor Company

Consolidated Results of Operations for the Years Ended December 31
(Dollar amounts in millions except those stated on a per share basis)

	1979	1978
Sales	**$7,613.2**	**$7,219.2**
Costs:		
Inventories brought forward from previous year	1,522.3	1,288.6
Materials, supplies, services purchased, etc.	4,360.9	3,968.5
Wages, salaries, and contributions for employee benefits	2,262.6	2,158.6
Depreciation (portion of original cost of buildings, machinery, and equipment allocated to operations)	311.8	257.1
Interest on borrowed funds	134.0	105.8
Taxes based on income (note 5)	233.9	396.9
	8,825.5	8,175.5
Deduct: Inventories carried forward to following year	1,670.2	1,522.3
Costs allocated to year (1)	7,155.3	6,653.2
Profit of consolidated companies	457.9	566.0
Equity in profit of affiliated companies (note 9)	30.2	(.8)
Profit of subsidiary credit companies	3.5	1.1
Profit for year — consolidated	**491.6**	**566.3**
Profit employed in the business at beginning of year	2,578.1	2,173.6
	3,069.7	2,739.9
Dividends paid	181.5	161.8
Profit employed in the business at end of year	$2,888.2	$2,578.1
Profit per share of common stock (note 6):		
Assuming no dilution	$ 5.69	$ 6.56
Assuming full dilution	$ 5.50	$ 6.33
Dividends per share of common stock	$2.100	$1.875

(1) Includes cost of goods sold: 1979 — $6,172.3; 1978 — $5,583.7

Report of Independent Accountants

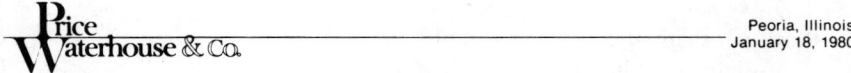

Peoria, Illinois
January 18, 1980

TO THE SHAREHOLDERS OF CATERPILLAR TRACTOR CO.:

In our opinion, the accompanying statements 1 through 5 present fairly (a) the financial position of Caterpillar Tractor Co. and consolidated subsidiaries at December 31, 1979 and 1978, the results of their operations and the changes in financial position for the years then ended, in conformity with generally accepted accounting principles consistently applied and (b) the historical financial data included therein. Our examinations of the statements for the years 1979 and 1978 were made in accordance with generally accepted auditing standards and accordingly included such tests of the accounting records and such other auditing procedures as we considered necessary in the circumstances. We have made similar annual examinations since incorporation of the company.

Price Waterhouse & Co.

single most important figure in the annual report, for it is one response to his question: "What has the company's management done for me this past year?"

4. The sales figure of $7,613.2 million represents the total billings made to customers of Caterpillar and its wholly owned subsidiary companies for sales of products and services in 1979. That these billings were not all collected in 1979 is indicated by the balance of $692.7 million "Receivable from customers and others" at December 31, 1979, shown on Statement 2 reproduced on page 99.

5. The "costs allocated to year" of $7,155.3 million were determined in Statement 1 by:

Adding:	Costs incurred during 1979 for	
	Materials, supplies, services purchased, etc..........	$4,360.9
	Wages, salaries and contributions to employees.....	2,262.6
	Depreciation (portion of original cost of buildings, machinery, and equipment allocated to operations)....................	311.8
	Interest on borrowed funds..................	134.0
	Taxes based on income.....................	233.9
		$7,303.2
To:	Inventories brought forward from previous year...	1,522.3
		$8,825.5
Less:	Inventories carried forward to following year......	1,670.2
Giving:	Costs allocated to year.....................	$7,155.3

This presentation of "costs allocated to year" is unique with Caterpillar. In its Form 10-K filed with the Securities and Exchange Commission, Caterpillar uses a more conventional presentation. A condensed "Consolidated Statement of Income," taken from the 10-K form, is shown next.

	1979
Net Sales.................................	$7,613.2
Cost of goods sold.........................	6,172.3
	1,440.9
Deduct:	
Selling, general, and administrative expense.......	689.8
Other expenses (net).......................	59.3
	$ 749.1

	691.8
Taxes based on income............................	233.9
Profit of consolidated companies..................	457.9
Equity in profit of affiliated companies and profit of subsidiary credit companies.............	33.7
Net Profit for Year	$ 491.6

Depreciation for the year, shown at $311.8 for 1979 in Statement 1, is included in cost of goods sold ($283.8) and in selling, general, and administrative expense (28.0) in the 10-K statement of income. Caterpillar explains "Depreciation" in Note 1C, reproduced on page 100.

6. In Statement 1, the company combines the statement of retained earnings with its statement of income by:

Adding:	Profit for year—consolidated.......	$ 491.6 million
To:	Profit employed in the business at the beginning of the year	2,578.1 million
		3,069.7 million
Less:	Dividends paid	181.5 million
Giving:	Profit employed in the business at end of year	$2,888.2 million

The $2,888.2 million figure for "profit employed in the business at end of year" appears also, of course, on the statement of financial position for December 31, 1979 (Statement 2); and the beginning-of-the year figure, $2,578.1 appears on the statement of financial position for December 31, 1978.

7. Although Statement 1 is a statement for the year 1979, it does not show all that happened in the operation of Caterpillar during the year. It doesn't show how much cash was taken in, how much cash was spent, or the change in cash during the year. It doesn't show how much the company spent for new buildings and equipment. It doesn't show how much money the company borrowed during the year. It doesn't show that the company issued additional capital stock during the year. In short, it *shows only what happened to the stockholders' interest in the corporation as a result of (1) sales to customers less related costs and expenses and (2) dividends to the stockholders.*

8. The comparative statements of income for 1979 and 1978 show:

Sales increased .... from $7,219.2 in 1978 to $7,613.2 in 1979 or 5.5%	$394.0 million
While costs allocated to year increased. .... from $6,653.2 in 1978 to $7,155.3 in 1979 or 7.5%	502.1 million
So that net income (exclusive of equity in profit of affiliated companies and credit companies) decreased................................... from $566.0 in 1978 to $457.9 in 1979 or 19.1%	108.1 million

In its 1979 Annual Report (page 38) the company's management analyzed "1979 vs. 1978" as follows:

> Net sales in 1979 were $7,613.2 million, a 5.5% increase over the $7,219.2 million in 1978. The increase was due to higher selling prices directly attributable to inflationary cost increases, partially offset by a decrease in physical volume of approximately 5%. This decrease resulted from a fourth-quarter 1979 strike by the United Auto Workers union. As a result of the strike, the company incurred a loss from operations in the fourth quarter of 1979.
>
> The decrease in physical volume for the year was a significant factor contributing to the reduction in gross margin (from 22.7% to 18.9%.) Gross margin was also adversely affected by the continued weakening of the U.S. dollar and by higher depreciation, start-up, and other costs associated with the company's capital expenditure program.
>
> Higher operating costs were incurred at some subsidiaries outside the United States, as costs in local currencies translated into more U.S. dollars due to higher rates of exchange. This weakening of the U.S. dollar adversely affected profit when selling prices could not be increased proportionately. While the effect cannot be precisely measured, the amount is estimated to be in excess of $20 million after tax.
>
> Interest expense increased from $111.9 million to $139.1 million due principally to increased short-term borrowings that were needed primarily to finance higher receivables, inventories and capital expenditures. Depreciation expense increased 21.3 percent due to significant capital expenditures during 1978 and 1979. Payroll taxes increased from $128.1 million to $153.1 million primarily because of higher employment and wage rates, and social security tax increases.

STATEMENT OF FINANCIAL POSITION

The statement of financial position shows what the corporation owned (assets), what it owed (liabilities), and the remainder (stockholders' equity) as of midnight of the stated date of the statement. It is a still picture of how the corporation stood at that point in time according to the generally accepted accounting principles for such a statement.

Let us look at Statement 2, Caterpillar's comparative statements of financial position as of December 31, 1979 and December 31, 1978. Observe that:

1. Caterpillar presents its consolidated financial position at December 31, 1979, by showing the following items.

Current Assets totaling...................		$2,606.9 million
Less:	Current Liabilities totaling.........	1,386.1 million
Giving:	Net Current Assets of.............	1,220.8 million
Plus:	Noncurrent Assets totaling.........	2,796.4 million
		4,017.2 million
Less:	Noncurrent Liabilities of..........	951.9 million
Giving:	Net Assets of..................	$3,065.3 million
Equal to:	Ownership consisting of:	
Common stock of.......................		$ 177.1 million
Profit employed in the business.............		2,888.2 million
Total stockholders' equity................		$3,065.3 million

2. This same information is presented by most companies in a statement called the balance sheet, in which the assets of the corporation are shown to equal liabilities plus owners' equity. Here is a balance sheet presentation of these figures.

CATERPILLAR TRACTOR COMPANY
Balance Sheet (using summary figures)
December 31, 1979

ASSETS		LIABILITIES AND OWNERS' EQUITY	
Current Assets.....	$2,606.9	Current Liabilities.........	$1,386.1
Noncurrent Assets ..	2,796.4	Noncurrent Liabilities	951.9
		Total Liabilities.........	$2,338.0
		Owners Equity	3,065.3
	$5,403.3		$5,403.3

Statement 2: Caterpillar Tractor Company

Consolidated Financial Position at December 31
(Millions of dollars)

	1979	1978
Current assets:		
Stated on basis of realizable values:		
Cash	$ 58.4	$ 51.0
Short-term investments	88.8	193.5
Receivable from customers and others (note 7)	692.7	767.8
Prepaid expenses and income taxes allocable to the following year	96.8	93.7
	936.7	1,106.0
Stated on basis of cost using principally "last-in, first-out" method:		
Inventories (note 1B)	1,670.2	1,522.3
	2,606.9	2,628.3
Deduct: Current liabilities:		
Notes payable (note 10)	404.2	112.6
Payable to material suppliers and others	789.5	853.5
Taxes based on income	133.4	236.7
Long-term debt due within one year	59.0	34.3
	1,386.1	1,237.1
Net current assets (statement 3)	1,220.8	1,391.2
Buildings, machinery, and equipment — net (notes 1C and 8)	2,571.7	2,218.5
Land — at original cost	66.1	62.9
Investments in affiliated companies (notes 1A and 9)	71.3	47.3
Investments in and advances to subsidiary credit companies (notes 1A and 9)	14.0	11.5
Deferred taxes based on income	23.5	(23.9)
Other assets	49.8	62.6
Total assets less current liabilities	4,017.2	3,770.1
Deduct: Long-term debt due after one year (note 11)	951.9	1,018.0
Net assets	$3,065.3	$2,752.1
Ownership (statement 4):		
Preferred stock of no par value (note 12):		
Authorized shares: 5,000,000		
Outstanding shares: none		
Common stock of no par value (note 13):		
Authorized shares: 105,000,000		
Outstanding shares: 1979 — 86,433,701; 1978 — 86,364,757	$ 177.1	$ 174.0
Profit employed in the business	2,888.2	2,578.1
	$3,065.3	$2,752.1

See notes

Notes to Financial Statements

1. Summary of significant accounting policies

A. Basis of consolidation

Caterpillar Tractor Co. has investments in subsidiaries, all of which are wholly owned, and in two affiliated companies, which are 50% owned. The accompanying financial statements include the accounts of Caterpillar Tractor Co. and all of its subsidiaries except its two credit subsidiaries. These credit subsidiaries are accounted for by the equity method; accordingly, their profit is included in the consolidated results of operations as a separate item and the consolidated financial position reflects the cost of the company's investments in and advances to these subsidiaries plus the profit retained by them. The affiliated companies are also accounted for by the equity method.

Note 9 contains combined financial information of the affiliated companies and the credit subsidiaries.

B. Inventories

With minor exceptions, inventories are stated on the basis of the "last-in, first-out" method of inventory valuation. This method was first adopted for the major portion of inventories in 1950.

If the "first-in, first-out" method had been in use, inventories would have been $1,655.3 million and $1,388.0 million higher than reported at December 31, 1979 and 1978, respectively.

Notes continued

C. Depreciation

Depreciation is computed principally using accelerated methods ("sum-of-the-years-digits" and "declining-balance") for both income tax and financial reporting purposes. These methods result in a larger allocation of the cost of buildings, machinery, and equipment to operations in the early years of the lives of assets than does the straight-line method. If the straight-line method had always been in use, "Buildings, machinery, and equipment — net" would have been $428.9 million and $370.1 million higher than reported at December 31, 1979 and 1978, respectively, and depreciation expense for 1979 and 1978 would have been, respectively, $59.8 million and $47.1 million less.

For financial reporting purposes the depreciation rates used worldwide are principally based on the "guideline" lives established by the U.S. Internal Revenue Service. For income tax purposes the depreciation rates used are principally based on the "guideline" lives for assets acquired prior to 1971 and on the Class Life ADR System for additions after 1970.

When an asset becomes fully depreciated, its cost is eliminated from both the asset and the accumulated depreciation accounts.

D. Interest on borrowed funds

All interest costs are charged against operations as incurred.

E. Investment tax credits

Investment tax credits are accounted for on the "flow-through" method for both income tax and financial reporting purposes. This method recognizes the benefit in the year in which the assets giving rise to the credits are placed in service.

2. Foreign exchange

Exchange gains or losses result from translating certain foreign currency assets and liabilities to U.S. dollars when the relationship between the foreign currency and dollar changes. Exchange gains or losses also result from the conversion of one currency for another or the settlement of a receivable or payable at a rate different from that at which the item was recorded.

Profit for 1979 included net exchange gains of $5.2 million ($1.7 million after tax) and profit for 1978 included net exchange losses of $19.9 million ($10.9 million after tax).

3. Research and engineering costs

Research and engineering costs related to the company's products are charged against operations as incurred. Such costs totaled $283.0 million and $256.1 million in 1979 and 1978, respectively. Of these amounts, $190.5 million in 1979 and $163.0 million in 1978 were attributable to new product development and major improvements to present products. The remainder was attributable to engineering costs incurred during the early production phase as well as ongoing efforts to improve present products.

4. Pension plans

The parent company and its subsidiaries have plans covering substantially all employees. Total pension expense for the years 1979 and 1978 was $151.8 million and $133.7 million, respectively. It is the company's policy to fund pension expense as it accrues.

The computed value of vested benefits exceeded the amount of pension funds at December 31, 1979 by approximately $445 million. The value of vested benefits is an actuarially determined amount representing the present value of the benefits expected to be paid to employees to the extent of their vested rights at the determination date. The excess of the value of the vested benefits over the amount of pension funds results primarily from increases in pension costs related to prior service, which are amortized and funded over periods not to exceed 30 years.

5. Taxes based on income

Taxes charged against operations comprise the following:

	1979	1978
	(Millions of dollars)	
Taxes currently paid or payable	$271.6	$395.9
Tax effect of timing differences	(37.7)	1.0
Taxes based on income	$233.9	$396.9

The timing differences relate primarily to pension expense, unrealized profit excluded from inventories, asset lives used for determining depreciation, and capitalization policy for certain tooling.

Taxes based on income were less than would result from applying the U.S. statutory rate to profit before tax for the reasons set forth in the following reconciliation:

	1979	1978
	(Millions of dollars)	
Taxes based on income computed at 46% (1979) and 48% (1978)	$318.2	$462.2
Increases (decreases) in taxes resulting from:		
Subsidiaries subject to tax rates other than 46% (1979) and 48% (1978)	$(2.3)	$(33.1)
Investment tax credits (note 1E)	(71.8)	(44.1)
Benefit of Domestic International Sales Corporations	(32.8)	(12.2)
State income taxes — net of federal tax	14.0	17.8
All other — net	8.6	6.3
	(84.3)	(65.3)
Taxes based on income	$233.9	$396.9

During 1979, two matters related to examinations of certain prior years' tax returns by the U.S. Internal Revenue Service were resolved. The first resulted in the capitalization, for income tax purposes, of certain tooling items previously charged to expense for both financial reporting and income tax purposes. This increased investment tax credits recorded in 1979 by $17.9 million. The second matter related to the company's successful litigation of a dispute concerning the qualification of a Domestic International Sales Corporation (DISC). This resulted in additional DISC benefits recorded in 1979 of $23.4 million.

U.S. taxes on income, net of foreign taxes paid or payable, have been provided on the undistributed profits of subsidiaries and affiliated companies, except in those instances where such profits have been permanently invested and are not considered to be available for distribution to the parent company. In accordance with this policy, the consolidated "Profit employed in the business" at December 31, 1979 included approximately $700 million of undistributed profits of subsidiaries and affiliated companies on which U.S. taxes on income, net of foreign taxes paid or payable, have not been provided. If for some reason not presently contemplated such profits were to be remitted or otherwise become subject to U.S. income tax, available credits would reduce the amount of tax otherwise due.

6. Profit per share information

Profit per share of common stock (assuming no dilution) is computed using the weighted average number of shares outstanding during the respective periods.

Profit per share of common stock (assuming full dilution) gives effect to the potential conversion of the 5½% Convertible Subordinated Debentures (convertible into common stock at $50.50 per share) and unexercised stock options.

7. Receivable from customers and others

Receivables at December 31, 1979 included $63.7 million evidenced by promissory notes from dealers and customers. Approximately $25.7 million of these notes mature beyond one year but were included in current assets in accordance with the accounting practice followed within the industry.

8. Buildings, machinery, and equipment — net

Buildings, machinery, and equipment — net at December 31, by major classification, were as follows:

Annual Reports to Stockholders

	1979	1978
	(Millions of dollars)	
Buildings	$1,472.8	$1,298.7
Machinery and equipment	2,736.9	2,338.3
	4,209.7	3,637.0
Deduct Accumulated depreciation	1,638.0	1,418.5
Buildings, machinery, and equipment — net	$2,571.7	$2,218.5

The company had commitments for the purchase or construction of fixed assets amounting to approximately $635 million at December 31, 1979. Capital expenditure plans are subject to continuous monitoring and changes in such plans could reduce the amount committed.

9. Investments in unconsolidated companies

Affiliated companies

The company's investments in affiliated companies consist of 50% interests in Caterpillar Mitsubishi Ltd., Japan ($70.0 million), and in Tractor Engineers Limited, India ($1.3 million). The other 50% owners of these companies are, respectively, Mitsubishi Heavy Industries, Ltd., Tokyo, Japan, and Larsen & Toubro Limited, Bombay, India.

Combined financial information of these affiliated companies for their most recent fiscal years, as translated to U.S. dollars, is as follows:

	September 30,	
	1979	1978
Financial Position	(Millions of dollars)	
Assets		
Current assets	$661.9	$670.2
Land, buildings, machinery, and equipment — net	108.4	96.8
Other assets	33.2	39.1
	803.5	806.1
Deduct Liabilities		
Current liabilities	472.8	530.5
Long-term debt (including subordinated debentures)	142.6	131.0
Other liabilities	43.1	48.0
	658.5	709.5
Ownership	$145.0	$ 96.6
Company share of ownership — 50%	$ 72.5	$ 48.3
Intercompany adjustments	(1.2)	(1.0)
Investments in affiliated companies	$ 71.3	$ 47.3

	Years ended September 30,	
	1979	1978
Results of Operations	(Millions of dollars)	
Sales	$901.3	$721.9
Profit after tax	$ 60.8	$ (1.1)
Company share of profit — 50%	$ 30.4	$ (.6)
Intercompany adjustments	(.2)	(.2)
Equity in profit of affiliated companies	$ 30.2	$ (.8)

Profit after tax for the combined affiliated companies in 1979 and 1978 would have been approximately $43.7 million and $26.2 million, respectively, if exchange gains and losses were excluded. The intercompany adjustments result primarily from the exclusion of unrealized profit from inventory.

Certain products are sold to and purchased from the affiliated companies at intercompany prices. In addition, the company received license fees under a license agreement with Caterpillar Mitsubishi Ltd. The total amount of these transactions with the affiliated companies was not material in relation to consolidated results of operations.

Credit subsidiaries

The two credit subsidiaries, Caterpillar Credit Corporation (U.S.) and Caterpillar Overseas Credit Corporation S.A. (Switzerland), assist dealers in the financing of sales of the company's products. At December 31, 1979, the total assets of these two companies were $63.4 million.

10. Short-term debt

The company has arrangements with several U.S. and non-U.S. banks to provide short-term lines of credit. These credit lines, which averaged $791 million (U.S. $367 million and non-U.S. $424 million) during 1979, are changed as the company's anticipated needs vary and are not indicative of the company's short-term borrowing capacity.

The company maintains compensating balances with U.S. banks which average 10% of the total U.S. lines of credit. Compensating balances maintained for the credit lines outside the U.S. were negligible.

Average month-end short-term borrowings during 1979 were $375 million and the approximate weighted average interest rate, significantly influenced by borrowings in Brazil, was 17.1%. At December 31, 1979, the company had confirmed short-term credit lines totaling $800 million of which $709 million was unused. Of the unused portion, $314 million was considered as support for outstanding commercial paper borrowings.

11. Long-term debt

Debt due after one year at December 31 consisted of the following:

	1979	1978
By parent company:	(Millions of dollars)	
Notes — 8.375% due 1982	$100.0	$ 100.0
Debentures — 5.125% due 1981-1986	14.5	14.5
Debentures — 5.30% due 1981-1992	90.0	97.5
Debentures — 6.875% due 1981-1992	76.0	82.0
Debentures — 8.60% due 1985-1999	150.0	150.0
Debentures — 8.75% due 1985-1999	100.0	100.0
Debentures — 8.0% due 1987-2001	200.0	200.0
Debentures — 5.50% due 1986-2000 — convertible subordinated	199.7	199.7
Other	7.8	7.9
By subsidiaries:		
Equivalent to	13.9	66.4
Long-term debt due after one year	$951.9	$1,018.0

The foregoing long-term debt at December 31, 1979 was payable as follows:

	(Millions of dollars)
1981	$ 27.6
1982	116.7
1983	16.5
1984	16.5
1985-1989	230.4
1990-1994	227.6
1995-1999	185.7
2000-2001	130.9
	$951.9

12. Preferred stock

The Board of Directors is authorized to issue up to 5,000,000 shares of preferred stock in series and to determine the number of shares and the dividend, conversion, voting, redemption, liquidation, and other terms of each series. As of December 31, 1979, none of the shares had been issued.

13. Stock options

In April 1970 and April 1977, shareholders approved plans providing for the granting to officers and other key employees of options to purchase common stock of the company. Options granted under both plans carry prices equal to the market price on the date of grant.

Stock appreciation rights may be granted as part of 1977 Plan options or as separate rights to holders of options previously granted under the 1977 Plan. A stock appreciation right permits an option holder to surrender an exercisable option or portion thereof and receive in exchange shares of common stock, cash, or a combination of both. The aggregate amount to be received will have a value equal to the excess of the fair market value of one share of stock, at the date of surrender, over the

Notes continued

option price multiplied by the number of shares covered by the option or portion thereof surrendered.

Changes during 1979 in shares subject to issuance under options were as follows:

	Shares
Options outstanding at December 31, 1978	1,140,623
Exercised	(69,485)
Lapsed	(4,700)
Options outstanding at December 31, 1979	1,066,438
Comprising:	
At average price of $31.59 per share	86,688
At average price of $44.54 per share	254,350
At average price of $55.48 per share	725,400
	1,066,438

No options were granted during 1979. At December 31, 1979, authority existed to grant future options for 477,350 common shares under the 1977 Plan.

14. Litigation

The company is a party to litigation matters and claims which are normal in the course of its operations, and while the results of litigation and claims cannot be predicted with certainty, based on advice of counsel, management believes that the final outcome of such matters will not have a materially adverse effect on the consolidated financial position.

15. Segment information
Business segments

The company is engaged in the manufacture and sale of earthmoving, construction, and materials handling machinery and equipment (Machinery and Equipment), such as track-type tractors, bulldozers, rippers, track and wheel loaders, lift trucks, pipelayers, motor graders, wheel dozers, compactors, wheel tractor-scrapers, hydraulic excavators, log skidders, off-highway trucks and related parts and equipment. The company also manufactures diesel engines for incorporation in its machines, and diesel and natural gas engines for sale as on-highway truck engines, marine and industrial engines, electric power generation systems, and related parts and equipment (Engines). Data on these business segments are as follows:

	1979	1978	1977
	(Millions of dollars)		
For the years ended December 31			
Sales to unaffiliated customers			
Machinery and equipment	$6,475.5	$6,162.5	$5,077.7
Engines	1,137.7	1,056.7	771.2
Transfers between business segments			
Engines	542.6	576.5	487.7
Eliminations	(542.6)	(576.5)	(487.7)
Consolidated sales	**$7,613.2**	**$7,219.2**	**$5,848.9**
Operating profit			
Machinery and equipment	$ 817.0	$ 956.3	$ 804.3
Engines	124.4	234.0	155.6
Eliminations	8.9	(1.3)	3.9
	950.3	1,189.0	963.8
General corporate expenses	(204.5)	(168.3)	(131.6)
Interest on borrowed funds	(134.0)	(105.8)	(95.4)
Miscellaneous income	80.0	48.0	40.3
Taxes based on income	(233.9)	(396.9)	(334.1)
Equity in profit of unconsolidated companies	33.7	3	2.1
Profit for year — consolidated	**$ 491.6**	**$ 566.3**	**$ 445.1**
Capital expenditures			
Machinery and equipment	$ 473.8	$ 377.4	$ 329.3
Engines	182.6	145.9	168.4
General corporate	19.5	20.1	18.7
	$ 675.9	$ 543.4	$ 516.4
Depreciation			
Machinery and equipment	$ 205.9	$ 173.7	$ 151.4
Engines	99.1	79.0	57.4
General corporate	6.8	4.4	1.7
	$ 311.8	$ 257.1	$ 210.5

At December 31			
Identifiable assets			
Machinery and equipment	$3,778.4	$3,427.9	$2,911.1
Engines	1,332.1	1,200.4	1,012.1
Eliminations	(15.7)	(24.6)	(23.3)
	5,094.8	4,603.7	3,899.9
General corporate assets	223.2	368.6	373.2
Investments in unconsolidated companies	85.3	58.8	72.5
Total assets	$5,403.3	$5,031.1	$4,345.6

The major portion of transfers between business segments occurs within the parent company. Transfer values reflect cost and a proportionate share of total operating profit. The high degree of integration of the company's manufacturing operations necessitates the use of a substantial number of allocations in the preparation of the business segment information.

Geographic segments

Manufacturing activities are carried on in 14 plants in the United States, three in the United Kingdom, two each in Brazil and France, and one each in Australia, Belgium, Canada, and Mexico. Four major parts warehousing and distributing facilities are located in the United States and eight are located abroad.

The product of manufacturing operations located outside the United States in most instances consists of components manufactured or purchased abroad which are assembled with components manufactured in the United States and transferred at intercompany prices. As a result, the profits of these operations do not bear any definite relationship to their assets. The company's intercompany pricing philosophy is that prices between Caterpillar companies are established at levels deemed equivalent to those which would prevail in arm's length transactions.

Data on the company's geographic segments, based on the location of the manufacturing operation, are as follows:

	1979	1978	1977
	(Millions of dollars)		
For the years ended December 31			
Sales to unaffiliated customers			
United States	$5,982.1	$5,905.7	$4,740.0
Europe	1,115.7	917.1	773.8
All other	515.4	396.4	335.1
Transfers between geographic areas			
United States	147.6	149.6	161.8
Europe	4.7	5.2	5.9
All other	1.9	1.2	—
Eliminations	(154.2)	(156.0)	(167.7)
Consolidated sales	**$7,613.2**	**$7,219.2**	**$5,848.9**
Operating profit			
United States	$ 871.6	$1,114.0	$ 872.5
Europe	46.9	61.3	77.4
All other	30.8	14.8	15.0
Eliminations	1.0	(1.1)	(1.1)
	950.3	1,189.0	963.8
General corporate expenses	(204.5)	(168.3)	(131.6)
Interest on borrowed funds	(134.0)	(105.8)	(95.4)
Miscellaneous income	80.0	48.0	40.3
Taxes based on income	(233.9)	(396.9)	(334.1)
Equity in profit of unconsolidated companies	33.7	.3	2.1
Profit for year — consolidated	**$ 491.6**	**$ 566.3**	**$ 445.1**
At December 31			
Identifiable assets			
United States	$4,054.5	$3,712.9	$3,150.1
Europe	642.2	538.3	486.4
All other	413.0	378.7	284.3
Eliminations	(14.9)	(26.2)	(20.9)
	5,094.8	4,603.7	3,899.9
General corporate assets	223.2	368.6	373.2
Investments in unconsolidated companies	85.3	58.8	72.5
Total assets	$5,403.3	$5,031.1	$4,345.6

Annual Reports to Stockholders

Data on the company's sales outside the United States, based on dealer location, are as follows:

	Europe	Africa, Middle East	Canada	Latin America	Australasia	Sales outside United States
	(Millions of dollars)					
1979						
Export sales of U.S. manufactured product	$ 488.5	$579.6	$427.5	$476.4	$527.9	$2,499.9
Sales of non-U.S. manufactured product	664.8	380.6	77.4	239.7	236.1	1,598.6
Total	$1,153.3	$960.2	$504.9	$716.1	$764.0	$4,098.5
1978						
Export sales of U.S. manufactured product	$ 412.9	$496.6	$370.1	$505.8	$398.7	$2,184.1
Sales of non-U.S. manufactured product	519.0	370.0	61.7	168.1	166.7	1,285.5
Total	$ 931.9	$866.6	$431.8	$673.9	$565.4	$3,469.6
1977						
Export sales of U.S. manufactured product	$ 340.5	$508.9	$279.1	$438.2	$290.9	$1,857.6
Sales of non-U.S. manufactured product	398.3	375.9	53.5	161.8	119.4	1,108.9
Total	$ 738.8	$884.8	$332.6	$600.0	$410.3	$2,966.5

Sales outside the United States were 53.8% of consolidated sales in 1979, 48.1% in 1978, and 50.7% in 1977.

16. Changing price levels (required supplementary information — unaudited)

The following information on constant dollar restatement of the company's consolidated profit and other financial data is prepared and presented in accordance with Statement of Financial Accounting Standards No. 33 — *Financial Reporting and Changing Prices*.

Adjustments to profit

Constant average 1979 dollars have been used as the basis to restate consolidated profit to reflect the estimated effects of general inflation. Most revenues and expenses, by occurring relatively uniformly throughout the year, are assumed to be approximately the same in nominal dollars and constant average dollars.

In the company's circumstances, the only profit component requiring restatement is depreciation — that portion of the original cost of buildings, machinery, and equipment allocated to operations. Those original costs, incurred over a number of years, were stated in dollars having various units of purchasing power. Depreciation has been restated in constant average 1979 dollars by using the changes in the Consumer Price Index for all Urban Consumers (CPI-U) to represent the rate of general inflation. The restatement is based upon the same methods, useful lives, and salvage values used for nominal dollar depreciation.

Inventory related expenses included in cost of goods sold are virtually the same in nominal dollars and constant average dollars because of the use of the "last-in, first-out" method of inventory valuation (note 1B).

Taxes based on income have not been restated since current tax laws do not permit adjustments to recognize the effects of general inflation. As a result, the effective income tax rate for 1979 increased from 33.8% on a nominal dollar basis to 38.8% on a constant dollar basis.

The company's financial accounting policies and methods tend to reflect the effects of general inflation in the determination of the results of operations. As a result, the adjustment to restate consolidated profit in constant average 1979 dollars is relatively minor.

Purchasing power gain on monetary items

When prices are increasing, the holding of cash and claims to cash results in a loss of general purchasing power because a given amount of money will buy less at the end of a year than it would have bought at the beginning of the year. Similarly, liabilities are associated with a gain of general purchasing power because the amount of money required to settle the liability represents a decreasing amount of purchasing power. These gains and losses of purchasing power (net) have been computed using the CPI-U and are shown below as "Gain from decline in purchasing power of net monetary liabilities."

Adjustments for changes in the general purchasing power of the U.S. dollar for the year ended December 31, 1979
(Millions of dollars)

Profit for year — consolidated (statement 1)			$491.6
Adjustments to restate costs for the effects of general inflation			
Depreciation — Cost of goods sold		$(81.6)	
— Other		(8.0)	(89.6)
Profit restated in constant average 1979 dollars			$402.0
Gain from decline in purchasing power of net monetary liabilities, in constant average 1979 dollars			$153.1

Five-year summary

The following five-year information has been adjusted, based on changes in the CPI-U, to restate nominal dollars to constant average 1979 dollars. Adjustments have been made to net assets presented in Statement 2 for inventories, land, buildings, machinery, and equipment. Differences between values for the other components of net assets expressed in terms of nominal dollars and constant dollars are insignificant.

Notes continued

**1975-1979 data adjusted for changes in
the general purchasing power of the U.S. dollar**

	Years ended December 31.				
	1975	1976	1977	1978	1979
Millions of constant average 1979 dollars:					
Sales	$6,694.2	$6,429.3	$7,005.8	$8,032.0	$7,613.2
Profit — consolidated	478.4	427.0	469.4	557.1	402.0
Net assets at year-end	3,889.3	4,195.1	4,557.3	5,019.6	5,368.8
Gain from decline in purchasing power of net monetary liabilities	78.3	57.4	137.5	103.4	153.1
Constant average 1979 dollars:					
Per share of common stock					
Profit assuming no dilution	$ 5.57	$ 4.96	$ 5.44	$ 6.45	$ 4.65
Dividends	$ 1.66	$ 1.86	$ 1.89	$ 2.09	$ 2.10
Market price at year-end	$60.79	$72.34	$64.10	$62.95	$51.09
Average consumer price index	161.2	170.5	181.5	195.4	217.4

17. Replacement cost (unaudited)

The Securities and Exchange Commission requires the computation and disclosure of the replacement cost of inventories and productive capacity (buildings, machinery, and equipment) and the related impact on cost of sales and depreciation.

The company has applied the "last-in, first-out" valuation method to the major portion of its inventories since 1950. Therefore, the replacement cost of inventories would be higher than the inventory value recorded in the accounts. Cost of sales based on replacement cost, however, would approximate the cost of sales using the "last-in, first-out" method of inventory valuation.

The replacement cost of productive capacity would be higher than the historical cost of such assets and, accordingly, replacement depreciation would be higher.

This generalized statement on replacement cost is furnished pursuant to specific commission guidelines and reference should be made to the more detailed and quantitative replacement cost data included in the company's 1979 Form 10-K to be filed with the commission.

18. Selected quarterly financial data (unaudited)

Financial data for the interim periods of 1979 and 1978 were as follows (dollar amounts in millions except those stated on a per share basis):

	1979 Quarter				1978 Quarter			
	1st	2nd	3rd	4th	1st	2nd	3rd	4th
Net sales	$1,923.7	$2,136.7	$2,232.2	$1,320.6	$1,630.1	$1,843.7	$1,816.8	$1,928.6
Gross profit	394.7	461.5	471.6	113.1	380.7	437.7	408.7	408.4
Profit for period	132.3	165.1	167.8	26.4	119.4	150.2	139.2	157.5
Per share of common stock								
Profit assuming no dilution	$1.53	$1.91	$1.94	$ .31	$1.38	$1.74	$1.62	$1.82
Profit assuming full dilution	$1.48	$1.84	$1.87	$ .31	$1.34	$1.68	$1.55	$1.76
Dividends paid	$ .525	$ .525	$ .525	$ .525	$ .450	$ .450	$ .450	$ .525

Sales and profit for the fourth quarter of 1979 were adversely affected by an extended strike by the United Auto Workers union. As a result, the company incurred a loss from operations. However, this was more than offset by favorable income tax adjustments and profit from unconsolidated companies, principally Caterpillar Mitsubishi Ltd.

Annual Reports to Stockholders

Statement 3: Caterpillar Tractor Company

Changes in Consolidated Financial Position
(Millions of dollars)

	1979	1978
Additions to net current assets from:		
Operations:		
Profit for year	$ 491.6	$ 566.3
Items affecting profit for year, but not affecting net current assets:		
Depreciation	311.8	257.1
Deferred taxes based on income	(47.4)	(12.1)
Equity in profit of affiliated companies	(30.2)	.8
Profit of subsidiary credit companies	(3.5)	(1.1)
Net current assets provided from operations	722.3	811.0
Long-term debt	2.8	91.4
Capital assets sold or scrapped	4.2	2.8
Common stock sold for cash under stock options	3.1	4.5
Common stock issued upon conversion of convertible debentures	—	.3
Dividends from affiliated companies	6.0	7.1
Dividends from subsidiary credit companies	1.0	—
Reduction in advances to subsidiary credit companies	—	8.7
Reclassification of other assets	10.8	—
Other	5.7	(4.7)
	755.9	921.1
Reductions of net current assets for:		
Cash dividends	181.5	161.8
Land, buildings, machinery, and equipment	675.9	543.4
Long-term debt	68.9	84.4
Reclassification of receivables	—	36.8
	926.3	826.4
Increase or (decrease) in net current assets during year	**(170.4)**	**94.7**
Net current assets at beginning of year	1,391.2	1,296.5
Net current assets at end of year	$1,220.8	$1,391.2
Increase or (decrease) in components of net current assets:		
Cash and short-term investments	$ (97.3)	$ 35.1
Receivable from customers and others	(75.1)	119.7
Prepaid expenses and income taxes allocable to the following year	3.1	(12.5)
Inventories	147.9	233.7
Net change in current assets	(21.4)	376.0
Notes payable	291.6	25.3
Payable to material suppliers and others	(64.0)	175.8
Taxes based on income	(103.3)	58.5
Long-term debt due within one year	24.7	21.7
Net change in current liabilities	149.0	281.3
Increase or (decrease) in net current assets during year	**$ (170.4)**	**$ 94.7**

See notes

This statement says, in effect, that the corporation owns property totaling $5,403.3 million for two classes of people, creditors and stockholders, whose interests in the assets are $2,338.0 million and $3,065.3 million respectively.

3. Caterpillar shows the individual asset items in Statement 2 at a hodgepodge of valuations:

	SHOWN AT
Cash and receivables.	Realizable values
Inventories.	Last-in, first-out cost
Buildings, machinery, and equipment	Balance of original cost allocable to future operations
Land.	Original cost
Investment in affiliated companies and subsidiary credit companies.	Cost plus profit retained by affiliate or subsidiary

In 1947, Mr. W. Blackie, then Caterpillar vice-president, commented on the company's adoption of the *financial position* form:

> While the statement of financial position reflects totals which are, of themselves, useful it should nevertheless be thoroughly understood that these totals are composed of elements which are not homogeneous. Recognition of this accounting fact is, in our opinion, fundamental to any proper interpretation of the statement, and it is particularly important that readers realize the limited extent to which current realization values find a place among the conventional and historical bases for asset accounting.[1]

Note: Compare Mr. Blackie's comments with the basic concepts of *going concern* and *historical dollar accounting*.

4. The company explains its basis of stating inventories in Note 1B, duplicated on page 99. While Caterpillar uses the last-in, first-out (LIFO) method of allocating costs against sales revenues, many other companies use other methods, such as first-in, first-out (FIFO), or average. Such differences in cost allocation methods between companies illustrate the basic concept of *diversity in accounting*

---

[1] *Financial Statements for Corporate Annual Reports*, by W. Blackie, *The Journal of Accountancy*, March, 1947.

among independent entities. And the further fact that Caterpillar has used last-in, first-out consistently from January 1, 1950, illustrates the basic concept of *consistency between periods for the same entity.*

5. The company shows "Buildings, machinery, and equipment—net" at $2,571.7 million for December 31, 1979. In Note 8, the company gives further details that we can summarize:

	December 31, 1979
Buildings, machinery, & equipment at original cost	$4,209.7 million
Deduct: Accumulated depreciation (portion of original cost allocated to operations to date) ..	1,638.0 million
Balance of original cost not allocated to operations to date	$2,571.7 million

The $4,209.7 million represents the dollar cost of buildings, machinery, and equipment acquired in many different years with dollars of varying purchasing power. The $2,571.7 million residual figure also represents dollars of varying purchasing power; it does not reflect either liquidating value or current replacement cost at December 31, 1979. Note again the effect of the basic concepts of *going concern* and *historical dollar accounting.*

Reproduced below is a note regarding replacement cost included in Caterpillar's 10-K report for 1979 filed with the SEC:

Replacement Cost (unaudited)

The Securities and Exchange Commission requires the computation and disclosure of the replacement cost of inventories and productive capacity (buildings, machinery and equipment) and the related impact on cost of sales and depreciation. The Commission anticipates that the replacement cost data will provide information not otherwise available in historical cost statements by demonstrating the impact of inflation and technological change on inventories and productive capacity. While the rules require the determination of replacement cost, generally accepted accounting principles to be followed in such computations have not been established.

There are inherent imprecisions in and general limitations on the usefulness of the replacement cost data being presented. The computations are based on several major hypothetical assumptions: (1) that the Company would replace its entire inventory and productive capacity at the end of its fiscal year; (2) that the funds were available to do so; (3) that such instantaneous replacements were physically possible; and (4) that such replacement would be accomplished without redesign, relocation or other attendant improvements.

The replacement data presented is not appropriate for use in determining economic income. In this hypothetical situation, the Company would expect substantial changes in other income determinants such as labor costs, maintenance and repairs, and utility costs which cannot reasonably be quantified and, therefore, these operating cost changes, which would result from the replacement of existing assets with assets of improved technology, are not reflected in the basic data provided. Also, because of the subjective judgments and specific circumstances involved, the data will not be fully comparable among companies and will be subject to variations in the methods of estimation employed.

Following is a summary comparison of the historical and replacement cost data for 1979 (in millions of U.S. dollars):

	Historical Cost	Replacement Cost
At December 31, 1979:		
Inventories....................	$1,670.2	$3,370.1
Buildings, machinery, and equipment (productive capacity)		
Gross amount	4,209.7	8,348.0
Undepreciated amount	2,571.7	4,320.1
For the Year Ended December 31, 1979:		
Cost of goods sold, including $283.8 of historical cost depreciation and $353.4 of replacement cost depreciation	$6,172.3	$6,231.7
Other depreciation expense	28.0	34.8

The Company follows a policy of eliminating the cost of an asset from both the asset and accumulated depreciation accounts when the asset becomes fully depreciated. The historical cost gross amount of Buildings, machinery and equipment does not include such fully depreciated assets still in service which had an historical cost of $457.7 million; however, those assets are included in the replacement cost gross amount of Buildings, machinery and equipment at an estimated replacement cost of $1,437.7 million. Included in both the gross and undepreciated amounts of Buildings, machinery and equipment for historical and replacement cost is $458.9 million of construction in process.

For historical cost purposes Inventories, with minor exceptions, are stated on the basis of the "last-in, first-out" method of inventory valuation. This method was first adopted for the major portion of inventories in 1950. Depreciation is computed principally using accelerated methods.

The replacement cost of Inventories was computed using December 1979 cost levels. Cost of goods sold (excluding depreciation) was computed based on the cost levels experienced at the time of sale.

The replacement cost of productive capacity (Buildings, machinery and equipment) was calculated by its various components. The replacement cost of buildings was computed by applying related published indices to the total of existing facilities by year of acquisition. The replacement cost of machinery and equipment was determined in two parts. First, machinery and equipment, by year of acquisition, was adjusted for inflation by applying indices to the respective major classes of equipment. Second, a further adjustment was made to the price-adjusted amount to reflect technological improvement. This overall degree of technological change was based on the Company's experience in replacing its productive capacity. Replacement cost depreciation was computed by applying the straight-line method to the average replacement cost. Asset lives used in computing historical cost depreciation were maintained for purposes of determining replacement cost depreciation.

6. Statement 2 shows that stockholders' equity at December 31, 1979, consists of:

Common stock (outstanding shares 86,433,701)	$ 177.1 million
Profit employed in the business	2,888.2 million
	$3,065.3

In a separate and unique statement, "Source of Consolidated Net Assets," Caterpillar shows a chronological summary, from 1925 through 1979, of how common stock and profit-employed-in-the-business (retained earnings) came to be shown at December 31, 1979, at $177.1 million and $2,888.2 million respectively:

Common stock:
Amount paid into the corporation by the stockholders
  (a) for shares issued at the formation of the
  corporation in 1925, and (b) for the additional
  shares issued since . . . . $ 119.8 million
Transfer from "profit employed" on account of
  stock dividends, stock split-ups, etc. . . . . 57.3 million
    Total for common stock at 12/31/79 . . . . $ 177.1 million

Profit employed in the business:
Total profit earned in the years 1925-1979. . . . . $4,828.5 million
Less: Cash dividends to stockholders $1,883.0
  Transfers to common stock on account of
  stock dividends, stock split-ups, etc. . . . . . . 57.3   1,940.3 million
Accumulated undistributed profit employed
  in the business at 12/31/79 . . . . $2,888.2 million

STATEMENT OF CHANGES IN FINANCIAL POSITION

The increases and decreases between the comparative statements of financial position as of December 31, 1978, and December 31, 1979, are summarized in the company's Statement of Changes in Financial Position for 1979, Statement 3.

The statement of changes in financial position summarizes significant financial *changes* that have occurred between the beginning and end of a company's accounting period. The statement is based upon comparative statements of financial position (balance sheets) at the current year-end and the previous year-end, and upon selected information taken from the statement of income and retained earnings for the current year and from other sources. The year's increases and decreases in various balance sheet items are rearranged according to the sources and application of funds. The concept of *funds* used in many corporation annual reports is *net current assets* (also called *working capital* or *net working capital*). This concept is used by Caterpillar in Statement 3.

Statement 3 shows that in 1979:

Additions to net current assets came from		
Net income before deduction of depreciation and other items (which did not involve an outlay of net current assets)........................		$722.3 million
Increase in long-term debt.....................		2.8 million
Miscellaneous sources.........................		30.8 million
		$755.9 million
Reductions of net current assets were required for		
Cash dividends................................	$181.5	
Additions to land, buildings, machinery and equipment..................................	675.9	
Reduction of long-term debt..................	68.9	$926.3 million
So net current assets decreased between December 31, 1978 and December 31, 1979..........		($170.4) million

The information presented in the statement of changes in financial position may be used to prepare a cash flow statement as discussed in Chapter 5.

AUDITOR'S OPINION

At the bottom of Statement 1 is a "Report of Independent Accountants" signed by Price Waterhouse & Co. This report is often referred to as the *auditor's opinion*.

The opinion states that:

1. The statements present "fairly" and "in conformity with generally accepted accounting principles."
2. These accounting principles were applied consistently.
3. The auditor's examination was made "in accordance with generally accepted *auditing* standards."

The opinion as presented for Caterpillar is an unqualified, or *clean*, opinion. If the auditor cannot give an unqualified opinion, he may give a qualified opinion, an adverse opinion, or a disclaimer of an opinion. Adverse opinions and disclaimers of opinions are rarely encountered in published annual reports.

SOME CONTROVERSIES IN CONTEMPORARY ACCOUNTING

Responsibility for Establishing Generally Accepted Accounting Principles

In late 1976, the Senate Subcommittee (Metcalf) on Reports, Accounting, and Management of the Committee on Government Operations issued a staff study that recommended, among other things, that financial accounting standards for publicly owned companies be established by the federal government.

In Chapter 1, we discussed the evolution of the various bodies responsible for establishing generally accepted accounting principles. Some people believe that neither the APB, the FASB, nor the SEC have taken the leadership role necessary to establish accounting standards or principles.

In 1980, the SEC had the authority to establish standards and the FASB, in effect, had the responsibility. The "Metcalf" report is sure to generate discussion and controversy over public and private sector responsibilities for years to come.

Objectives of Financial Statements

Many people have argued that it is difficult to establish accounting standards if the objectives of financial statements are not clearly defined. One of the first considerations of the FASB after its formation was a "Conceptual Framework for Financial Accounting and Reporting." In November 1978, the FASB issued a *Statement of Financial Accounting Concepts No. 1—Objectives of Financial Reporting by Business Enterprises*. The objectives in the Statement pertain to general external financial reporting and are not restricted to information cummunicated by financial statements. Later statements are expected to cover the elements of financial statements and their recognition, measurement, and display as well as other related matters such as unit of measurement.

Uniformity vs. Flexibility

Flexibility has been particularly bothersome to critics of the status of accounting standards. Critics say that there is too much leeway in the application of accounting standards, and that therefore the financial statements of different companies are not comparable. The proponents of flexibility argue that uniformity could lead to less comparability because of differences in the ways in which companies operate. Today, companies must disclose their accounting policies in their annual report, so there is some data available for putting statements of different companies on a comparable basis for analytical purposes.

Historical Cost and the Unit of Measurement

Inflation has been a major concern for businessmen and the accounting profession in recent years. As the inflation rate rose above 5 percent, more people realized that an inflationary environment affects business decisions and the reported results of these decisions.

In 1976, the SEC issued Accounting Series Release No. 190, which required certain companies to show, in a note or separate statement in their annual 10-K report, information pertaining to the replacement cost of inventories and property, plant, and equipment.

In September 1979, the FASB issued a *Statement on Financial Reporting and Changing Prices* (No. 33). This Statement requires public enterprises that have more than $125 million of inventories and gross properties, or more than $1 billion of assets, to disclose the effects of both general inflation and specific price changes as supplementary information in their published annual reports.

Caterpillar presented this supplementary information in Note 16. The FASB is now developing plans for evaluating the usefulness of information required by the Statement. Chapter 8 discusses, in greater detail, the requirements of this FASB Statement 33.

There is a common agreement that present financial statements based on historical cost are a mixture of "apples and oranges." However, there is no agreement on the common denominator for measurement. A significant amount of research on accounting for inflation is being done around the world. This research should lead to a better understanding of the implications of measuring economic activity in terms other than historical costs.

Materiality

The concept of materiality was discussed in Chapter 1. There has been no established criteria for what is material, and many have believed that this lack has allowed abuses in financial reporting, particularly in the area of appropriate disclosure. The FASB has issued a discussion memorandum on materiality that should lead to standards establishing criteria for determining materiality.

Interim Reporting

Traditionally, interim financial statements have not been *audited* statements and have not necessarily met the reporting standards of annual reports. The FASB has established a task force to reconsider APB Opinion No. 28, *Interim Financial Reporting*.

Pensions

Although APB Opinion No. 8 (1966) narrowed considerably the latitude in determining pension costs, many people still think that there is too much difference between the minimum and maximum standards established in APB Opinion No. 8. In March 1980, the FASB issued a *Statement of Accounting and Reporting by Defined*

Benefit Pension Plans (No. 35), and in May 1980, issued FASB Statement No. 36 on the disclosure of pension information. The FASB is doing further work in the pension area.

Other Controversies

A number of other areas are still considered unsettled and controversial. Among these are:

1. extraordinary items and prior period adjustments,
2. interperiod income tax allocation,
3. reporting for segments of a business,
4. earnings-per-share calculations, and
5. foreign currency translation.

A reader of current business periodicals will be familiar with these controversies. Many of the arguments for and against certain accounting treatments can be found in APB opinions and FASB publications.

SUMMARY

Corporations ordinarily issue to their stockholders and other interested parties annual reports summarizing activities of the past year and significant plans for the future. In addition to the financial statements, the annual report contains the auditor's opinion, which states that the underlying records have been examined and that the financial statements are presented fairly in conformity with generally accepted accounting principles applied on a consistent basis.

The notes to the financial statements are considered an essential part of the statement and are necessary for a complete and accurate interpretation of the information contained in the statements. The accounting policies of the company are disclosed in the footnotes, usually in the first note, and provide a starting point for an analysis of the financial statements.

7

Analysis of Financial Statements

This chapter discusses knowledge of the company and its environment, analysis of its cash flows, and calculation and interpretation of return-on-investment and nine other financial ratios.

Analysis of financial statements involves more than the perfunctory calculation of financial ratios. In this chapter we will stress the need of the analyst first to acquire a knowledge of the company and its environment and then to gain familiarity with the company's figure relationships in the preparation of the statements for analysis. For the statements of income and financial position, preparation requires rearranging, condensing, figure-rounding, and taking notes of significant figure relationships. For the statement of changes in financial position, a conversion to the cash flow statement form is followed by an analysis of the cash flows and an attempt to project them for the future. The balance of the chapter is devoted to the description, calculation, and interpretation of return-on-investment and nine other financial ratios. Throughout the chapter Caterpillar Tractor figures for 1977/1979 are used for illustration.

THE COMPANY AND ITS ENVIRONMENT

A review of the company's annual reports and SEC 10-K forms for several years reveals much about the nature of the company, its industry, and the environment in which it has operated. In the case of Caterpillar for the years 1977/1979, one discovers:

- The company was a multinational company with roughly one-half of its sales outside the United States.
- The company sold to 248 dealers, which in turn sold and serviced Caterpillar equipment to customers throughout the world.
- The company designed, manufactured, and marketed two product lines:
    Earthmoving construction and material handling machinery and equipment, and
    Diesel and natural gas engines for earthmoving and construction machines, on-highway trucks, etc.
- Inflation in the United States and abroad affected the company's operations and its financial statements:

    Sales of $7,219 million in 1978 were 23% higher than in 1977 with 40% of the increase attributable to higher prices and 60% of the increase to greater physical volume.

    Sales of $7,613 million in 1979 were 5.5% higher than in 1978, all of the increase, and more, being attributable to higher prices because physical volume decreased 5%.

    The decrease in physical volume in 1979 resulted from a fourth quarter strike by the United Auto Workers Union.

    The weakening of the United States dollar in both 1978 and 1979 adversely affected profits, in excess (after tax) of $30 million in 1978 and $20 million in 1979.

This brief review of Caterpillar's background and environment in 1977/1979 illustrates the kind of information needed. In order to do an adequate job of statement analysis, the analyst needs to learn as much as possible about the company and the environment that produced the statements being analyzed.

Analysis of Financial Statements 117

PREPARATION OF INCOME STATEMENT FOR ANALYSIS

The analyst should rearrange, condense, and figure-round a company's published statement of income and retained earnings to facilitate further analysis and, incidentally, to gain familiarity with the company's figures.

In the case of Caterpillar, we have used figures obtained from the company's 1979 and 1978 Annual Reports to prepare Illustration 7-1.[1]

Note, in Illustration 7-1, the figures have been rounded to millions in such a fashion that the figures within the statement "prove."[2] Note also that dollar figures for each year have been placed on a "percentage of sales" basis, and that supplemental data on the effect of changing prices (inflation) have been added at the bottom of the statement. Certain things stand out in Illustration 7-1:

- Cost of goods sold was a much higher percentage of sales in 1979 (81.1%) than in 1978 (77.4%) and in 1977 (77.0%). As a consequence, profit before taxes was 9.1% of sales in 1979 compared to 13.3% in 1978 and 1977.

   The company explains:[3]

   The fourth-quarter strike of the United Auto Workers Union was the principal reason for the decrease in profit. Profit for 1979 would have exceeded the 1978 level if the work stoppage had not occurred.

- Interest expense increased from $112 million in 1978 to $139 million in 1979 "due principally to increased short-term borrowings that were needed to finance higher receivables, inventories, and capital expenditures."[4]

- Income taxes were a smaller proportion of profit before taxes in 1979 than in 1978 and 1977. The company attributed the decrease in the effective income tax rate from 41.2% in 1978 to 33.8% in 1979 (1) to higher investment tax credits (arising from $675 million capital expenditures in 1979 compared to $543 million in 1978), and (2) to the decrease in the U.S. statutory rate from 48% to 46%.

---
[1] Compare to Statement 1 reproduced in Chapter 6.
[2] Statistical rounding, with a note that the figures do not "prove", is not appropriate.
[3] Page 8, Caterpillar's 1979 Annual Report.
[4] *Ibid.*, page 38.

Illustration 7-1

Caterpillar Tractor Company
Statement of Income and Retained Earnings For 1979, 1978, and 1977
(In millions of dollars)

	1979	1978	1977	Percentage of Sales 1979	1978	1977
Sales	7613	7219	5849	100.0	100.0	100.0
Cost of goods sold	6172	5584	4503	81.1	77.4	77.0
Interest expense	139	112	100	1.8	1.5	1.7
Selling and other expenses (net)	610	560	469	8.0	7.8	8.0
Total	6921	6256	5072	90.9	86.7	86.7
Profit before taxes	692	963	777	9.1	13.3	13.3
Income taxes	234	397	334	3.1	5.5	5.7
Profit of consolidated companies	458	566	443	6.0	7.8	7.6
Equity in profit of subsidiary and affiliated companies	34	-0-	2	0.4	-0-	-0-
Profit for year	492	566	445	6.4	7.8	7.6
Dividends	182	162	136	2.4	2.2	2.3
To retained earnings	310	404	309	4.0	5.6	5.3
Retained earnings:						
Beginning of year	2578	2174	1865			
End of year	2888	2578	2174			
MEMOS:						
Annual depreciation	312	257	210			
Per share figures:						
Profit (no dilution)	$5.69	$6.56	$5.16			
Dividends	2.10	1.875	1.575			
4th quarter figures:						
Sales	1321	1929	1518			
Cost of goods sold	1207	1520	1171			

ADDENDUM—Adjustments for Effects of Changing Prices (Inflation):

Pursuant to FASB Statement No. 33, the company reported its adjustments for changes in general purchasing power of the U.S. dollar for the year ended December 31, 1979 (millions of dollars):

Profit for year—consolidated (statement 1)	$492
Adjustment to restate costs for effects of general inflation	(90)
Profit restated in constant average 1979 dollars	$402
Gain from decline in purchasing power of net monetary liabilities, in constant average 1979 dollars	$153

- Dividends to stockholders were 37% of profit in 1979 compared to about 30% in 1978 and 1977. Over the ten-year period, 1970-79, the average payout percentage has been 34%. Nevertheless, dividends per share have shown a steady increase, from $.80 in 1970 to $2.10 in 1979.

- The company has since 1950 been using the LIFO inventory method so that, except for depreciation, its revenues and expenses have been pretty much on a current dollar basis each year. In 1979, historical cost depreciation of $312 million required an upward adjustment of $90 million to place it on a 1979 cost basis. Profit restated in "constant average 1979 dollars" became $402 million, compared to the $492 million reported. The $90 million adjustment for depreciation was more than offset by the $153 million "gain from decline in purchasing power of net monetary liabilities."

PREPARATION OF STATEMENT OF FINANCIAL POSITION FOR ANALYSIS

Caterpillar's statements of financial position for year-end 1979, 1978, and 1977, rearranged and figure-rounded, are shown in Illustration 7-2.

The rearrangement in Illustration 7-2 has condensed assets, liabilities, and owners' equity according to the following pattern:

Assets	*Liabilities*
Cash and cash equivalent	Payables and accruals
Trade receivables (net)	Liability for income taxes
Inventories	Short-term debt
Property, plant and equipment (net)	Long-term debt (due within a year and after)
Investments in affiliated and subsidiary companies	Deferred income taxes
All other assets	Other liabilities

Owners' Equity

Preferred stock
Common stock
Retained earnings

Since the distinction between current and noncurrent assets and lia-

Illustration 7-2

Caterpillar Tractor Company
Condensed Statements of Financial Position
12/31/79, 12/31/78, and 12/31/77
(In millions of dollars)

	12/31/79	12/31/78	12/31/77	Increase/(Decrease) 1978/79	1977/78
Cash and cash equivalent	147	244	209	(97)	35
Receivables (net)	693	768	648	(75)	120
Inventories	1670	1522	1288	148	234
Property, plant and equipment (net)	2638	2282	1999	356	283
Investments in affiliated & subsidiary companies	85	59	73	26	(14)
Other assets	147	156	129	(9)	27
	5380	5031	4346	349	685
Payables and accruals	790	854	678	(64)	176
Liability for income taxes	133	237	178	(104)	59
Short-term notes payable	404	112	87	292	25
Long-term debt (<&> 1 yr.)	1011	1052	1024	(41)	28
Deferred income taxes	(23)	24	36	(47)	(12)
Total liabilities	2315	2279	2003	36	276
Common stock	177	174	169	3	5
Retained earnings	2888	2578	2174	310	404
Owners' equity	3065	2752	2343	313	409
	5380	5031	4346	349	685
MEMO:					
Inventories at FIFO	3326	2910	2390		
Replacement cost reported to SEC pursuant to ASR 190:					
Inventories	3370	2957	2434		
Productive capacity (buildings, machinery, and equipment)	4320	3794	3230		
Excess of above over reported costs of inventories & buildings, machinery, and equipment (net)	3448	3010	2432		

bilities serves no useful statement analysis purpose, the distinction is ignored in Illustration 7-2. The figure rounding in Illustration 7-2

Analysis of Financial Statements

has been done in such a way that the figures within the statement prove. Percentage-of-total-assets figures have not been shown in Illustration 7-2 since inventories and fixed assets, stated on a past cost basis, make the total asset figure nonhomogeneous. Instead of percent-of-total figures, we have shown increase/decrease figures 1979 cf. 1978 and 1978 cf. 1977.

In Note B to its financial statements, Caterpillar shows how much higher its inventories stated at LIFO would be if stated on a first-in, first-out basis. In the "Memo" at the bottom of Illustration 7-2, Caterpillar's inventories calculated at FIFO are shown. Also shown in the "Memo" are the 12/31 replacement cost figures for inventories and "productive capacity" reported by Caterpillar to the Securities and Exchange Commission. The excess of replacement costs over reported figures is derived as follows:

	12/31/79	12/31/78	12/31/77
Inventories:			
Replacement cost	3370	2957	2434
Reported figures	1670	1522	1289
Excess	1700	1435	1145
Buildings, Machinery and Equipment (net):			
Replacement cost	4320	3794	3230
Reported figure	2572	2219	1943
Excess	1748	1575	1287
TOTAL EXCESS	3448	3010	2432

Several matters concerning Illustration 7-2 warrant brief comment:

- The UAW 4th quarter strike distorted 1979 year-end figures for normal comparisons. Because of the strike, there was a decrease of $608 million in 4th quarter sales from $1929 million in 1978 to $1321 million in 1979, and this decrease in sales explains the decreases in year-end receivables, payables and accruals, and income tax liability. The increase in year-end inventories raises a question.
- Many companies have used accelerated depreciation for income tax purposes, straight-line for financial reporting—and, as a consequence, have accumulated sizable amounts in their deferred tax liability account. Caterpillar has used accelerated depreciation for both income tax and financial reporting—so deferred

income tax has been a comparatively small amount for Caterpillar.

- The FIFO costs of inventories approximate year-end replacement costs. As one would expect, in an inflationary economy, replacement costs at year-end are slightly higher than FIFO.
- If we substitute the 12/31/79 replacement costs for inventories and "productive capacity" for the historical cost figures, we get:

	As Reported	Replacement Costs	Difference
Inventories	1670	3370	1700
Buildings, machinery & equipment (net)	2572	4320	1748
Cash, receivables, land, etc.	1138	1138	-0-
Total Assets	5380	8828	3448
Liabilities	2315	2315	-0-
Owners' Equity	3065	6513	3448
Total	5380	8828	3448

Note: The figures reported to the SEC are not altogether appropriate for this purpose. Caterpillar has deferred until 1980 disclosure of current cost information required by FASB Statement No. 33. See Chapter 8.

CONVERSION OF STATEMENT OF CHANGES IN FINANCIAL POSITION TO A CASH FLOW STATEMENT

Caterpillar's published statements of changes in financial position have been converted to a cash flow statement form[5] for 1979, 1978, and 1977. Illustration 7-3 shows also totals for the three years. Concerning Illustration 7-3, note:

- A careful analysis will indicate some of Caterpillar's problems of operating in an inflationary economy. Annual sales increased from $5042 million in 1976 to $7613 million in 1979, a 3-year increase of $2571 million—the increase in dollar sales attributable about 2/3rds to price increases, 1/3rd to increases in physical volume. The increase in sales was accompanied by a need to finance higher receivables, inventories, and capital expenditures.

[5] See Chapter 5.

Note the increases in year-end receivables and inventories over the 3-year period, broken only temporarily, for receivables, by the 4th quarter strike in 1979.

- A year-to-year inquiry into the factors accounting for "cash internally generated"—$686 million in 1977, $692 in 1978, $482 in 1979—is instructive. A 16% increase in dollar sales in 1977 brought Caterpillar's sales and profit to the then highest levels in the company's history. Net income before deduction of noncash depreciation, etc., was $678 million in 1977, but the increase in year-end receivables and inventories was only 5% and was offset by increases in payables and accruals, and income tax liability—so "cash internally generated" in 1977 was $686 million. In 1978 sales increased to $7219 million, profit to $566 million, and net income before depreciation to $811 million— all three record highs. Year-end receivables rose $120 million and inventories $234 million, and though offset in part by increases in payables and accruals ($176) and income tax liability ($59), the net sum of the four items was a negative $119 million. So "cash internally generated" in 1978 was $692 million— about the same as for 1977—though profit in 1978 was $121 million higher than in 1977. In 1979 annual sales increased 5% to $7613 million, though sales for the 4th quarter decreased 32% because of the UAW strike—despite the strike, profit for 1979, $492 million, and net income before depreciation, $722 million, were the second highest in Caterpillar's history.

Because of the decrease in 4th quarter sales (and profit), decreases in year-end receivables, inventories, payables and accruals, and income tax liability might have been expected. The strike was abnormal, however, and normal relationships were queered, especially as to inventories. However we may hypothesize, the fact is that the net sum of the four items was a negative $240 million, so "cash internally generated" was $482 million in 1979, $200 million less than in 1977 and 1978.[6]

---

[6] In this discussion of factors affecting "cash internally generated", it was necessary to compare 4th quarter sales only for 1979 because in 1976/78, 4th quarter sales were a stable 25%/27% of annual sales:

	Annual Sales (In Millions)	Fourth Quarter Sales	
		Amount (in millions)	% of Annual
1976	5,042	1,263	25.0
1977	5,849	1,518	26.0
1978	7,219	1,929	26.7
1979	7,613	1,321	17.4

Illustration 7-3

CASH FLOW STATEMENT
(Changes that decrease cash are shown in parentheses.)

Company Caterpillar Tractor Co. in Millions of Dollars	Year / Sales	1979	1978	1977	Total 3 Years
	Sales	7,613	7,219	5,849	—
Net Income		492	566	445	1503
Add: Depreciation		312	257	210	779
Add: Other noncash expenses–Deferred income taxes		(48)	(12)	25	(35)
Subtract: Noncash revenues–Equity in profit–affiliated and subsidiary companies		(34)	-0-	(2)	(36)
Net income before depreciation and other noncash expenses and revenues		722	811	678	2211
And this might have represented cash inflow but it did not happen this way because the company:					
a. Collected (less than) more than it billed customers, as shown in *Receivables* (increase) decrease		75	(120)	(43)	(88)
b. Bought and manufactured (more than) less than the cost of goods shipped, as shown in *Inventories* (increase) decrease		(148)	(234)	(44)	(426)
c. Paid out (more than) less than the costs it incurred, as shown in *Payables & Accruals* (decrease) increase		(64)	176	55	167

- For the 3-year period 1977-79 as a whole, the most striking thing about Caterpillar's cash flow statement was that the company was able to finance discretionary outgoes for dividends ($480) and net additions to property, plant and equipment ($1724), a total of $2204 million in large part from "cash internally generated," $1860 million. Resort to outside financing was in the form of short-term debt ($373). The company's use of "cash internally generated" to finance its large capital expenditures during the 1970s explains why dividend payout for the ten years has averaged only 34% of reported profit, as noted earlier.

- The cash flow statement model may be used for forecasting. In its 1979 Annual Report, Caterpillar forecasted "1980 sales expected to increase" and result in a physical sales volume "approximately equal to the 1978 level." Suppose we use forecasts

Illustration 7-3 continued.

d. Paid out (more than) less than income tax incurred, as shown in *Income Tax Liabilities* (decrease) increase	(103)	59	40	(4)
Total–Four Items	(240)	(119)	8	(351)
so that "cash internally generated" was	482	692	686	1860
There were "discretionary" outgoes of cash for: Acquisitions of property, plant and equipment (in excess of dispositions)	(671)	(540)	(513)	(1724)
Dividends to stockholders	(182)	(162)	(136)	(480)
Total Discretionary Outgoes	(853)	(702)	(649)	(2204)
Cash internally generated less discretionary outgoes	(371)	(10)	37	(344)
Financing and other cash inflows and outgoes were:				
Increase (decrease) in long-term debt (due <&> 1 yr.)	(41)	29	(39)	(51)
Increase (decrease) in notes payable	292	25	56	373
Issuance of common stock	3	4	6	13
Dividends from, and reduction in advances to, affiliated & subsidiary companies	7	16	9	32
Other	13	(29)	52	36
Total Financing and Other Flows	274	45	84	403
With the effect on the company's cash (and cash equivalent) being an increase (decrease) of	(97)	35	121	59

(in millions) for 1980: Sales $8500 (4th quarter $2000), profit $600, depreciation $360, dividends $180, capital expenditures (net) $650. Our forecast might then be brought together:

Net income (600) before depreciation (360)		960
Receivables increase (40% of 2,000 less 693)	(107)	
Inventories increase to 1,770 (guess)	(100)	
Payables and accruals increase (guess)	75	
Income tax liability increase (guess)	50	
Sum of four items		(82)
Cash internally generated		878
Discretionary outgoes:		
Capital expenditures (net)	(650)	
Dividends	(180)	
		(830)
Cash internally generated less discretionary outgoes		48

For statement analysis purposes, a number of cash flow statement forecasts may be made as forecasts of individual items are varied.

- It needs to be observed that the cash flow statements prepared from Caterpillar's traditional statements of income and financial position are valid without making the adjustments of profit, inventories, and fixed assets called for by FASB Statement No. 33. If, for 1979, we used the adjusted statements of income and financial position, we would show (in millions):

Reported profit of $492 less additional depreciation of $90	$402
Add: Depreciation—$312 plus 90	402
Deferred income taxes and equity in profit of affiliated and subsidiary companies	(82)
Net income before depreciation and other noncash expenses and revenues	$722

So there is no change from the $722 figure in Illustration 7-3. The adjustments to the 12/31/79 balance sheet represented an entry:

Inventories (A)	Incr	1700
Buildings, machinery and equipment (net) — (A)	Incr	1748
Owners' equity (OE)	Incr	3448

Since this entry does not affect cash, it would be reversed for the purpose of our cash flow statement.

RATIO ANALYSIS OF FINANCIAL STATEMENTS

Illustration 7-4 shows the calculation of a number of ratios for Caterpillar Tractor Company for 1979 and 1978, based upon figures taken from Illustrations 7-1 and 7-2.

Return-On-Investment Ratio

Return-on-investment (ROI), as used in this chapter, refers to the relationship between the *net income* of a company (or one of its divisions) and the *total assets* of the company (or its divisions) made available to management to produce the net income. The relationship may also be expressed as return-on-total-capital (ROTC) or as return-on-assets (ROA). The return-on-investment ratio is used to measure management performance at both the division and company levels. The reasoning is that management, either at the division or at the company level, is supplied with a total investment in assets—cash, receivables, inventories, plant and equipment, and other assets—and is expected to manage this total investment so as to earn a satisfactory return on it.

The ratio may be computed directly and simply by dividing net income by total assets. E.I. DuPont de Nemours Company pioneered the use of the two-step calculation which relates both net income and assets to sales as follows:

$$\frac{\text{Net Income}}{\text{Sales}} \text{ times } \frac{\text{Sales}}{\text{Total Assets}}$$

DuPont's practice has been adopted by many other companies. The two-step approach is used in Illustration 7-4.

Item 1-A-3 of Illustration 7-4 shows return-on-investment, calculated from Caterpillar's reported figures, declined from 12.0 percent in 1978 to 9.5 percent in 1979. The major cause was the decline in profit on sales (1-A-1), from 7.8 percent in 1978 to 6.5 percent in 1979—attributable for the most part to the 4th quarter strike in 1979. There was also a slight decline in the utilization of assets to produce sales, from 1.54 in 1978 to 1.46 in 1979.

The return-on-investment ratio should be used with care and judgment, for the ratio is usually derived from conventional accounting statements which have many limitations. Because of these limitations and because of the varying purposes for which the ratio may be used, variations in the computation of the ratio are encountered in practice.

When "investment" is defined as average total assets, the average may be computed by averaging total assets shown on the statements of financial position as of the beginning and end of the accounting period, as in Illustration 7-4. For seasonal businesses, average total assets may be more appropriately determined by averaging total assets shown in monthly or quarterly statements. In some cases, "investment" is taken to mean total assets shown on the balance sheet reduced:

1. By the amount of idle assets, or

Illustration 7-4

Caterpillar Tractor Company

Financial Ratios for 1979 and 1978 (Source: Illustrations 7-1 and 7-2)

	COMPUTATIONS		RATIOS	
	1979	1978	1979	1978
1. *Return-On-Investment*				
A-1. "Margin" (Profit ÷ Sales)	492/7613	566/7219	6.5%	7.8%
A-2. "Turnover" (Sales ÷ Avg. Total Assets)	7613 / (5380 + 5031)/2	7219 / (5031 + 4346)/2	1.46 Times	1.54 Times
A-3. R.O.I. (Margin × Turnover)	.065 × 1.46	.078 × 1.54	9.5%	12.0%
Based on Repl. Costs				
B-1. "Margin" (Adj. Profit ÷ Sales)	402/7613	Data Not	5.3%	N.A.
B-2. "Turnover" (Sales ÷ Adj. Total Assets)	7613 / (8828 + 8041)/2	Available in Ill. 7-1	0.9 Times	N.A.
B-3. Adj. R. O. I. (Margin × Turnover)	.053 × 0.9		4.8%	N.A.
2. *Receivable Collection Period*				
A. Avg. Daily Sales in 4th Quarter	1321 ÷ 92 Days	1929 ÷ 92 Days		
B. Year-End Receivables ÷ Avg. Daily Sales	693 ÷ 14.36	768 ÷ 20.97	48 Days	37 Days

3. *Inventory Turnover*				
A-1. Average Inventory – At LIFO	$(1670 + 1522)/2$	$(1522 + 1288)/2$		
A-2. Cost Goods Sold ÷ Avg. LIFO Inventory	$6172 \div 1596$	$5584 \div 1405$	3.9 Times	4.0 Times
Based on LIFO CGS and FIFO Inventory				
B-1. Average Inventory – At FIFO	$(3326 + 2910)/2$	$(2910 + 2390)/2$		
B-2. Cost Goods Sold ÷ Avg. FIFO Inventory	$6172 \div 3118$	$5584 \div 2650$	2.0 Times	2.1 Times
4. *Current Ratio At Year-End*				
Current Assets ÷ Current Liabilities	$2607 \div 1386$	$2628 \div 1237$	1.88 to 1	2.12 to 1
5. *L-T Debt to L-T Debt and Equity at Year-End*				
A. Based on Conventional Statement	$1011 \div 4076$	$1052 \div 3804$	25%	28%
B. Based on Repl.-Costs Adj. Statement	$1011 \div 7524$	$1052 \div 6814$	13%	15%
6. *Total Debt to Total Assets at Year-End*				
A. Based on Conventional Statement	$2315 \div 5380$	$2279 \div 5031$	43%	45%
B. Based on Repl.-Cost Adj. Statement	$2315 \div 8828$	$2279 \div 8041$	26%	28%
7. *Earnings on Common Equity*				
A. Based on Conventional Statement	$\dfrac{492}{(3065 + 2752)/2}$	$\dfrac{566}{(2752 + 2343)/2}$	16.9%	22.2%
B. Based on Repl.-Cost Adj. Statement	$\dfrac{402}{(6513 + 5762)/2}$	N.A.	6.5%	N.A.
8. *Earnings Per Share*				
Profit for Common ÷ Weighted Avg. No. of Shares	$492 \div 86.4$	$566 \div 86.3$	$5.69	$6.56
9. Book Value Per Share at Year-End	$3065 \div 86.43$	$2752 \div 86.36$	$35	$32
10. *Price/Earnings Ratio*				
Market Price (4th Qtr.) ÷ Earnings Per Share	$52 \div 5.69$	$57 \div 6.56$	9 Times	9 Times

2. By the amount of nonoperating assets, or
3. By the amount of assets financed by current liabilities.

Many companies define "investment" to include property, plant, and equipment at original cost rather than at original cost less accumulated depreciation. If we were to adopt this definition for Caterpillar Tractor Company, property, plant, and equipment at 12/31/79 would be figured at $4276 million instead of at $2638 million. DuPont's practice of including fixed assets at their undepreciated cost has no doubt influenced other companies to do so. One argument advanced for the practice is that it is a way of compensating for price level changes (inflation). A more direct way of adjusting for inflation is to use current replacement costs, as we have done in item 1-B, Illustration 7-4. Item 1-B-3 shows 1979 return on investment at 4.8 percent compared to 9.5 percent using conventional figures, primarily because "turnover" is 0.9 times using replacement costs compared to 1.46 using conventional figures.

The "return" numerator to be used in the return-on-investment calculation should be consistent with the "investment" denominator used. In the case of Caterpillar Tractor Company, an adjustment of reported net income by adding back the after-tax cost of interest on borrowed money may be in order. In the case of Caterpillar Tractor for 1979, we might add back $75 million after-tax interest[7] to the reported net income of $492 million; then, if we divided the $567 million adjusted income figure by the $5206 million investment, we would obtain an ROI of 10.9 percent, compared to the 9.5 percent without the adjustment for the after-tax cost of interest. Many of the questions concerning adjustment of the net income figure relate to (1) unusual and nonrecurring income, and income on nonoperating assets, and (2) interest expense, income taxes, and unusual and nonrecurring expenses.

In financial literature, the phrase "return-on-investment" is an expression used in many different contexts. Whenever a reader encounters "return-on-investment," he should determine:

1. What is meant by "return" and what is meant by "investment," as witness the various definitions discussed heretofore in this chapter.

---

[7] The company's incremental tax rate in 1979 was 46%. The after-tax cost of $139 million interest at 54%, 100%-46%, is $75 million.

2. Whether the return-on-investment is:
    a. Retrospective, as used for performance appraisal in this chapter, or
    b. Prospective, as used for project evaluation in capital budgeting decisions.

RECEIVABLE COLLECTION PERIOD, INVENTORY TURNOVER, AND CURRENT RATIO

Two observations regarding the receivable collection period are noteworthy: (1) 4th quarter sales when available are more reliable than annual sales for calculating this ratio, and (2) the number of days determined for this ratio can be compared with the company's credit terms, the company's previous experience, and with the collection period for similar companies. In Illustration 7-4, Item 2, we used 4th quarter sales to determine Caterpillar's period to be 48 days for 1979 compared to 37 days for 1978. Because of the 4th quarter strike in 1979, the 48-day period appears to be abnormal. The 37-day figure for 1978 is more typical.

The inventory turnover ratio is a useful and widely used ratio. Ideally, both the numerator, cost of goods sold, and the denominator, average inventory, should be at current costs. Caterpillar, using the LIFO method, shows cost of goods sold at current costs but inventories at past costs. Inventory turnover ratios for Caterpillar calculated on this basis, Item 3-A of Illustration 7-4, a turnover of 3.9 times for 1979, 4.0 times for 1978. Both figures are suspect, as the recalculation in Item 3-B using current cost FIFO inventory figures confirms. The Item 3-B turnover figures—2.0 times for 1979 and 2.1 times for 1978—are the more trustworthy.

The current ratio—current assets to current liabilities—is shown in Item 4, Illustration 7-4, 1.88 to 1 for 12/31/79 and 2.12 to 1 for 12/31/78. This ratio is of dubious value. The ratio would be meaningful to the short-term creditor only if the company is to be liquidated and the creditor could be assured of first call upon the liquidation proceeds. The liquidation concept, moreover, is contrary to going-concern basis upon which the balance sheet is prepared. The current ratio is of questionable value to management, for if management performance is being appraised by return-on-investment, the less current assets the company has, the higher the rate of return.

DEBT RATIOS

The ratio of long-term-debt to long-term-debt-and-equity measures the investment of bondholders relative to the investment of stockholders. The larger the ratio, the more the company is said to "trade on its equity." For Caterpillar, Item 5-A of Illustration 7-4 shows the ratio to be 25 percent at 12/31/79 and 28 percent at 12/31/78. The balance sheet figure for debt is on a current dollar basis but the equity figure is not, for Caterpillar's inventory and fixed assets are stated at past dollars with the result that equity is stated in part on past costs. So we have again the numerator, long-term debt, stated on one basis and the denominator stated on another. To correct this, Item 5-B shows equity reflecting replacement costs of inventories and fixed assets. Item 5-B shows the ratio to be 13 percent at 12/31/79, 15 percent at 12/31/78—both ratios indicating a small proportion of long-term debt in the "invested capital" of Caterpillar.

The ratio of total debt to total assets measures the interest of all creditors, not just bondholders, in the assets of the company. Again, the larger the ratio, the more the company "trades on its equity." For Caterpillar, Item 6-1 of Illustration 7-4 shows the ratio to be 43 percent at 12/31/79 and 45 percent at 12/31/78. The numerator again is stated at current costs, the denominator in part at past costs. To correct, Item 6-B reflects current replacement costs of inventories and fixed assets in stating fixed assets. The ratio then becomes 26 percent at 12/31/79 and 28 percent at 12/31/78. Included in Caterpillar's liabilities at 12/31/78 is Deferred Income Taxes, $24 million, a *de minimis* item, but for companies which have a sizable deferred income tax amount, two questions should be raised: Does deferred income tax represent a liability? Should it be considered a part of equity in computing debt/equity ratios?

STOCKHOLDERS' EQUITY AND EARNINGS RATIOS

The ratio of earnings on common equity is a measure of the return on common stockholders' investment, as stated on the company's balance sheet(s). The ratio is affected not only by the return-on-investment ratio but also by the extent to which the company uses debt and preferred stock as a means of financing its investment in assets. The more lower-cost debt is used, the more a company is said to "trade on its equity." And the more a company successfully "trades on its equity," the higher the return to its common stockholders. In the case of Caterpillar Tractor for 1979, the company used $2297 million funds provided by creditors, at an after-tax cost of $75 million, or about 3¼ percent; this enabled the company to earn 16.9 percent on its common stockholders' investment, when its overall ROI was 10.9 percent (adjusted for after-tax cost of interest). The profit-on-common-equity ratio is subject to many of the limitations noted for the return-on-investment ratio. These will not be repeated here.

Earnings per share is based upon the net income figure reported in the income statement and is subject, therefore, to all of the limitations of that statement. AICPA APB Opinion No. 15 provides, in paragraph 12, that "earnings per share or net loss per share data should be shown on the face of the income statement." APB Opinion No. 15 further provides, in paragraph 47, that "computations of earnings per share should be based on the weighted average number of common shares and common share equivalents outstanding during each period presented." Computation of earnings-per-share is relatively simple when a company has no "potentially dilutive convertible securities, options, warrants or other rights that upon conversion or exercise could in the aggregate dilute earnings per common share." When a company does not have these complicating factors, the computation is made by dividing net income available for common shares by the weighted average number of common shares. When a company has both common and preferred shares outstanding, with the preferred being nonconvertible into common, net income is reduced by the amount of preferred dividends in order to determine "net income available for common shares." The computation of Caterpillar's earnings per share is shown in Item 8 of Illustration 7-4–$5.69 for 1979 and $6.56 for 1978–assuming no dilution from potential conversion of convertible debentures and unexercised stock options.

Book value per share is based upon the figures reported in the balance sheet, and is subject, therefore, to all of the limitations of that statement. Many of these limitations were noted in the discussion of return-on-investment, and will not be repeated here. The extent of these limitations, for a particular company, is indicated by the difference between the book value of the company's stock and its market value, if the stock is publicly traded. Note the difference between the book value of Caterpillar's common shares, $35 at 12/31/79, and the market value $52 (in 4th quarter, 1979). For a closely held company, one whose stock is not publicly traded, care should be taken that book value is not equated with fair market value.

The price/earnings ratio is based upon the net income figure reported in the income statement and is subject, therefore, to all the limitations of that statement. It is difficult to measure net income for a single year with preciseness. Additional difficulties are encountered when there are extraordinary items or "potentially dilutive convertible securities, options, warrants or rights"; in such circumstances, one needs to be careful in selecting the earnings-per-share figure for the purpose of computing the price/earnings ratio. Moreover, when we relate today's market price to earnings-per-share for a past period, we are doing something which is somewhat illogical, for presumably an investor buys stock for its *future*, not its *past*, earnings. As a matter of cash exchange, a buyer of stock puts out cash today for his expectations of future cash dividends and the future market price for the stock.

SUMMARY

To do an adequate job of statement analysis, the analyst needs to review the company's annual reports, 10-K forms, and other sources to learn what he can about the company and the environment that produced the statements being analyzed. Both to facilitate his analysis and to gain familiarity with the company's figures, the analyst should rearrange, condense, and figure-round the company's published statements of income, retained earnings, and financial position. The analyst all the while should make notes of:

- Economic developments affecting the company during the period covered.
- The company's accounting policies and practices,
- Supplementary data provided, and
- Figure relationships of special interest.

The company's statement of changes in financial position should be converted to the cash flow statement form explained in Chapter 5,

Analysis of Financial Statements

and then that statement should be carefully analyzed and a forecast (or forecasts) of the cash flow statement attempted.

Ratios such as those included in Illustration 7-4 should be calculated and interpreted. A summary of the ten ratios included in Illustration 7-4 follows:

Return-On-Investment (ROI) may be determined by dividing profit by investment, or by multiplying profit on sales by "turnover" of investment. ROI is used to measure management performance at both the division and company levels. ROI can be improved by increasing the percentage of profit on sales or by improving "turnover." Many companies consider *investment* to be average total assets on their balance sheets. Some companies begin with this figure and add back accumulated depreciation so that, in effect, fixed assets are included at original cost. Other companies consider investment to be total assets less current liabilities. Adjustments may be made for price changes (inflation). The *profit* numerator in the ROI calculation should be consistent with the concept of investment employed. Thus, profit may be net income or net income before income taxes, with possible adjustments for interest expense, gain (or loss) from nonoperating assets, and unusual and nonrecurring items affecting income. The return-on-investment ratio should be used with care and judgment, since it is derived from conventional accounting statements which have many limitations. Whenever a reader encounters the expression "return-on-investment" in financial literature, he should seek to determine from the context (1) what is meant by "return" and what is meant by "investment" and (2) whether the return-on-investment measure is *retrospective* as in performance appraisal, or *prospective* as in project evaluation in capital budgeting.

The relationship between sales and receivables is shown by the *receivable collection period*. If appropriate consideration is given to seasonal and other fluctuations in sales, to elimination of any cash sales, and to the presence of any unusual account balances in the year-end receivable figure, the receivable collection period can be the most trustworthy of all the ratios described in this chapter. The relationship between cost of goods sold and average inventory is shown by the *inventory turnover ratio*. Appropriate consideration needs to be given to any difference between the basis on which cost of goods sold is stated and the basis on which average inventories are stated. When cost of goods sold is stated on a current-cost LIFO basis, then average inventories stated on a current-cost FIFO basis should be used in figuring the inventory turnover ratio. The *current ratio* is a ratio which, though readily calculated and frequently cited, is of no value to management and is dubious value even to the short-term creditor.

The relationship between debt and equity may be expressed by the *long-term-debt to long-term-debt-and-equity ratio*, and by the *total-debt to total-assets ratio*. The debt figure should be a fairly valid "current-dollar" figure. The equity figure when derived from a conventional balance sheet is subject to the limitations of that statement.

Equity and earnings ratios include earnings on common equity, earnings per share, book value per common share, and price/earnings ratio. These ratios also are subject to the limitations of the conventional accounting statements from which they are derived. Earnings-per-share computations are complicated when there are potentially dilutive convertible securities, options, warrants or similar securities.

8

Accounting for Changing Prices

The purpose of this chapter is to discuss how certain public enterprises report the effects of changing prices in their external financial reports. We will discuss the features of traditional financial statements and examine the objectives of financial reporting by business enterprises in relation to the changing business environment. We will next discuss the disclosure requirements of FASB Statement No. 33, Financial Reporting and Changing Prices, and will show how two large public enterprises presented this supplementary information. We will conclude the chapter by discussing the usefulness of financial information adjusted for changing prices.

TRADITIONAL FINANCIAL STATEMENTS

In the years since 1970, the United States has experienced a period of rapidly rising prices. In fact, prices as measured by the Consumer Price Index doubled from the beginning of 1970 to the beginning of 1980. This condition of overall rising prices is referred to as inflation. Before proceeding to accounting for changing prices, we will discuss the features of traditional financial statements.

A dominant feature of traditional financial statements is the measurement of the historical cost of inventories, property, plant and equipment, and intangible assets. These assets normally constitute a high proportion of the total assets of most business enterprises and this is the reason why conventional accounting is commonly referred to as "the historical cost model."

A second feature is the reliance of traditional financial statements on exchange transactions at historical costs. Most exchange transactions are recorded at historical costs, but many of them are not. For example, sales and accounts receivables are measured on the basis of historical exchange costs. However, when these costs are adjusted for estimated uncollectibles, they represent their net realizable values and not their historical costs.

A third feature is the use of a variety of current value measurements, which include replacement cost (under lower-of-cost-or-market rule), net realizable value (trade accounts receivables), and present value of expected cash flows (long-term receivables and long-term liabilities). A departure from the use of historical cost to improve financial reports includes the use of the equity method of accounting for unconsolidated subsidiaries and certain other investments.

The departure from the total use of historical costs for financial statements came about through the efforts of the accounting profession and interested related organizations in their attempts to convey meaningful and useful financial information to various decision makers. In the next section, we examine some objectives of financial statements.

Objectives of Financial Reporting by Business Enterprises

In November 1978, the Financial Accounting Standards Board issued a *Statement of Financial Accounting Concepts No. 1: Objectives of Financial Reporting by Business Enterprises*. In that Statement, it is suggested that financial reporting should provide:

- Information that is useful to present and potential investors and creditors and other users in making rational investment, credit and similar decisions.

- Information to help present and potential investors and creditors and other users in assessing the amounts, timing and uncertainty of prospective cash receipts from dividends or interest and the proceeds from the sale, redemption, or maturity of securities or loans.
- Information about the economic resources of an enterprise, the claims to those resources, and the effects of transactions, events, and circumstances that change its resources and claims to those resources.

The Statement goes on to state that financial reporting is expected to provide information about an enterprise's financial performance, and hence the primary focus of financial reporting is information about earnings and its components. The objectives of financial reporting, however, stem largely from the information needs of external decision makers who have a wide range of interests. Some of these interests are not related to earnings.

Financial accounting is not designed to measure directly the value of a business enterprise, but the information it provides may be helpful to those who wish to estimate its value. This is related to one of the objectives—that financial reporting should provide information about how management of an enterprise has discharged its stewardship responsibility to owners (stockholders) for the use of the enterprise resources entrusted to it. Management is accountable for the efficient and profitable use of these resources and for protecting them to the extent possible from unfavorable economic impacts of factors in the economy such as inflation or deflation. The users of financial reports need to have an understanding of the effects of changing prices on a business enterprise to make decisions regarding investing, lending, and other matters.

FINANCIAL REPORTING AND CHANGING PRICES

Financial statements in the United States have traditionally been prepared using historical costs. Because the statements reflect dollar amounts which have resulted from transactions taking place over a period of years, the purchasing power of the dollars shown in the statements is not the same. A plant built in 1970 does not show on the balance sheet in dollars that are equivalent in purchasing power to the dollars shown on the same balance sheet for a plant built in 1980.

Because of the rapid inflation since 1970, the accounting profession and interested related organizations have been concerned with methods of accounting for inflation. The Accounting Standards Steering Committee of the United Kingdom and Ireland issued in January 1973, Exposure Draft 8: *Accounting for Changes in the Purchasing Power of Money* and in May 1974, issued a provisional statement of Statement Accounting Practice No. 7 with the same title. In 1975, the British government Committee on Inflation Accounting, named the "Sandilands Committee" after its chairman, recommended an entirely different approach which it called "current cost accounting."

In December 1974, the FASB issued an Exposure Draft also calling for certain supplementary disclosures based on financial reporting in units of general purchasing power using an overall measure of inflation, the GNP Implicit Price Deflator, to measure purchasing price changes. In 1976, the Securities and Exchange Commission (SEC) issued Accounting Series Release No. 190 that required the disclosure of certain inventory and property replacement costs for large nonfinancial companies, commencing with 1976 financial statements. The FASB proposal was withdrawn after the SEC issued its replacement cost requirement.

In September 1979, the FASB issued *Statement of Financial Accounting Standards No. 33: Financial Reporting and Changing Prices*. Statement No. 33 applies only to large public corporations having:

1. Total Assets of $1 billion or more after deducting depreciation, or
2. Inventory plus gross property, plant and equipment of $125 million or more.

The Statement establishes standards for reporting both general inflation (constant dollar accounting) and changes in specific prices (current cost accounting). The term "general inflation" means a rise in the general level of prices or a decline in the general purchasing power of the monetary unit. Since conventional financial statements are recorded in nominal dollars, there is no direct allowance for the variability of the dollar's purchasing power. The presentation of certain financial information in units having the same general purchasing power may be useful to decision makers and the method used to compute that information is called "constant dollar accounting." The method used to compute changes in specific prices is called "current cost accounting."

In the introduction to Statement No. 33, the FASB states that it is intended to help users of financial statements in the following ways:

1. Assessment of future cash flows
2. Assessment of enterprise performance
3. Assessment of the erosion of operating capability
4. Assessment of the erosion of general purchasing power

There is general agreement that the effects of changing prices should be taken into consideration in interpreting financial statements. There has not been general, agreement on how to measure the change in prices. Thus, Statement No. 33 requires *supplementary disclosure* of certain information intended to show the effects of changing prices. The Statement does not change the standards of financial accounting and reporting used in the preparation of the customary historical cost financial statements. The supplementary disclosures were required to be included in annual reports for years ending on or after December 25, 1979. (Current cost information could be deferred until the 1980 annual report.)

The major provisions of the Statement require the following disclosures for the current year:

1. Adjustments for general inflation using an average-for-the-year constant dollar basis. The index to be used in computing information on a constant dollar basis is the Consumer Price Index for all Urban Consumers (CPI-U). Appendix A contains the CPI-U from 1919-1979.
2. Adjustments for current costs that may be based on specific price indices, current costs of comparable assets, or other measurement techniques.
3. A statement of income from continuing operations adjusted for the effects of changing prices on both a constant dollar and current cost basis.
4. The purchasing power gain or loss on net monetary items.
5. The current cost amounts of inventory and property, plant

and equipment at the end of the fiscal year.
6. Holding gains or losses on inventory and property, plant and equipment during the year.

There are also additional requirements for disclosure of selected financial data for the five most recent fiscal years. They include the following:

1. Net sales and other operating revenues at historical cost and adjusted to a constant dollar basis.
2. Income (loss) from continuing operations adjusted for the effects of changing prices on both a constant dollar and current cost basis.
3. Income (loss) per common share from continuing operations on a constant dollar and current cost basis.
4. Net assets at fiscal year-end on a constant dollar and current cost basis.
5. Increase or decrease in current cost amounts of inventory and property, plant and equipment held during the year, net of inflation.
6. Purchasing power gain or loss on net monetary items.
7. Cash dividends per common share adjusted to a constant dollar basis.
8. Market price per common share at fiscal year-end adjusted to a constant dollar basis.

FINANCIAL STATEMENT PRESENTATION

FASB Statement No. 33 requires no changes in the basic financial statements. The required information is to be presented in supplementary statements, schedules, or supplementary notes in financial reports.

In Exhibit 1, General Electric Co. showed the effects of changing prices in its 1979 annual report as supplementary information. Shell Company has published price level adjusted financial information each year since 1974 and presented the supplementary information as shown in Exhibit 2.

The FASB realized the difficulties of standardizing presentation and has written the Statement to provide more flexibility than is customary in Board Statements. It encourages experimentation within the guidelines of the Statement and the development of new techniques that fit the particular circumstances of the enterprise. This has resulted in some variations in the presentation of the supplementary information on the effects of changing prices, especially for enterprises of different industries.

In December 1979, the FASB published *Illustrations of Financial Reporting and Changing Prices* to help companies apply Statement No. 33 and disclose information on changing prices. The publication portrays the effects of changing prices on various types of enterprises and reflects the views of management in assessing the impact on their business operations.

It should be noted that application to income producing real estate properties and unprocessed natural resources have not yet been resolved adequately at the time of this writing. Such companies are not required to disclose current cost information about such assets (the assets are exempted but not the companies). There are no special exemptions from requirements to disclose information on a historical cost/constant dollar basis.

LIMITATIONS AND USEFULNESS OF FINANCIAL INFORMATION ADJUSTED FOR CHANGING PRICES

The special characteristics of an industry can be important factors in determining the kind of information that is most useful for assessing the effects of changing prices. This is particularly so for enterprises which own assets subject to high technological changes. There is difficulty in obtaining an accurate current cost of such assets; the greater the degree or rate of technological changes affecting an enterprise's equipment or product, the less accurate will be the current cost computation.

In its first year of introduction, many shortcomings were detected in implementing the Statement that have led to certain confusion and hamper a clear understanding of financial information adjusted for changing prices. A major shortcoming is the failure of Statement No. 33 to require a comprehensive restatement for constant dollar information. This has resulted in the different treatments accorded

EXHIBIT 1: General Electric Co.

Financial issues: the impact of inflation

Inflation is commonly defined as a loss in value of money due to an increase in the volume of money and credit relative to available goods and services, resulting in a rise in the level of prices. Inflation in the U.S. is generally recognized to be caused by a combination of factors, including government deficits, sharp increases in energy costs, and low productivity gains including the effect of proliferating government regulations.

Although loss of purchasing power of the dollar impacts all areas of the economy, it is particularly onerous in its effect on savings — of both individuals in forms such as savings accounts, securities and pensions, and of corporations in the form of retained earnings.

For the individual, with inflation of 6% a year, the dollar saved by a person at age 50 will have lost three-fifths of its value by the time the person is age 65. With a 10% inflation rate, almost four-fifths of the dollar's value is lost in 15 years. This problem affects almost everyone, including those presently working and especially those who are on fixed incomes.

The situation is rendered even more difficult by the progressive income tax system. A Congressional staff study reports that a family of four with an income of $8,132 in 1964 would need a 1979 income of $18,918 to have kept pace with the increase in the Consumer Price Index over the years. However, the 1979 income of $18,918 puts the family into a higher tax bracket which, when coupled with increased Social Security taxes, reduces real after-tax income $1,068 below the equivalent 1964 level.

Your Company and all U.S. businesses face a similar problem. Business savings are in the form of retained earnings — the earnings a company keeps after paying employees, suppliers and vendors, and after payment of taxes to government and dividends to share owners. If a company is to continue in business, much less grow, it must be able to save or retain sufficient earnings, after providing a return to its share owners, to fund the cost of replacing — at today's inflated prices — the productive assets used up. Retention of capital in these inflationary times under existing tax laws is a challenge facing all businesses.

U.S. tax regulations permit recognition of the impact of inflation on a company's inventory costs by use of the LIFO (last-in, first-out) inventory method. In general, under the LIFO method, a company charges off to operations the current cost of inventories consumed during the year. With inflation averaging over 11% last year, the negative impact on operations of using current costs with respect to a supply of goods is substantial. Financial results are portrayed more accurately when the LIFO method is used in periods of high inflation, and GE has used LIFO for most of its U.S. manufacturing inventories for a quarter-century. The Statement of Earnings on page 32 is on that basis. As supplementary information to that Statement of Earnings: use of the LIFO method increased 1979 and 1978 operating costs by $430.8 million and $224.1 million (to $20,330.7 million and $17,695.9 million), respectively, with a corresponding reduction of reported pre-tax profits.

Unfortunately, U.S. tax regulations fail to provide an equivalent to LIFO for the impact of inflation on a company's costs of property, plant and equipment. Instead, deductions for wear and tear on these assets are based on original purchase costs rather than today's replacement costs. In general, the resulting shortfall must be funded from after-tax earnings.

The supplementary information shown in Table 1 restates operating results to eliminate the major effects of inflation discussed above. Table 1 compares GE operating results as reported on page 32 with results adjusted in two ways. First, results are restated to show the effects of general inflation — the loss of the dollar's purchasing power — on inventories and fixed assets. The second restatement shows results restated for changes in specific prices — the current costs of replacing those assets. Your management feels that the last column in Table 1 is the more meaningful and has therefore shown, in Table 2 on page 30, five years of results on that basis, also adjusted to equivalent 1979 dollars to make the years comparable. While the techniques used are not precise, they do produce reasonable approximations.

In these earnings statements, specific adjustments are made to (1) *cost of goods sold* for the current cost of replacing inventories and (2) *depreciation* for the current costs of plant and equipment. The restatements for inventories are relatively small because GE's extensive use of LIFO accounting already largely reflects current costs in the traditional statements. However, a substantial restatement is made for the impact of inflation on fixed assets, which have relatively long lives. The $624 million of depreciation as traditionally reported, when restated for general inflation, increases to a total of $880 million. But the restatement necessary to reflect replacement of these assets at current costs grows to $980 million. The net effect of these restatements lowers reported income of $6.20 a share to $4.68 on a general inflation-adjusted basis and $4.34 on a specific current cost basis.

It is significant to note that for the five years 1975-1979, even after adjustment for inflation, your Company has shown real growth in earnings and a steady increase in share owners' equity over the entire period. After adjusting earnings for current costs and restating all years to equivalent 1979 dollars, your Company's average annual growth rate in real earnings was 21% since 1975 and 8% since 1976. This means that the growth in GE's earnings has been real, not just the product of inflation.

An important insight from these data is depicted in the pie charts at right. These show that, over the five years 1975-1979, because of inflation 10% more of GE's earnings were taxed away than appeared to have been the case using traditional financial statements. While the traditional earnings statements indicated an effective tax rate of 41% over this period, the "real" tax rate averaged 51% of profits before taxes. Consequently, earnings retained for growth were cut in half to 16% of income before tax, not 32% as reflected in the traditional financial statements. Over the period, share owners received a measure of protection against inflation's impact as about two-thirds of after-tax earnings were distributed — equivalent to an average annual growth rate of about 8% in *real* dividends.

An area receiving special attention by management is experimentation with the use of inflation-adjusted measurements at the individual business and project level for capital budgeting. Since 1973, your Company has been experimenting with various techniques to measure the im

General Electric Co.
Table 1: supplementary information – effect of changing prices (a)

(In millions, except per-share amounts)   The notes on page 30 are an integral part of this statement.

For the year ended December 31, 1979	As reported in the traditional statements	Adjusted for general inflation	Adjusted for changes in specific prices (current costs) (b)
Sales of products and services to customers	$22,461	$22,461	$22,461
Cost of goods sold	15,991	16,093	16,074
Selling, general and administrative expense	3,716	3,716	3,716
Depreciation, depletion and amortization	624	880	980
Interest and other financial charges	258	258	258
Other income	(519)	(519)	(519)
Earnings before income taxes and minority interest	2,391	2,033	1,952
Provision for income taxes	953	953	953
Minority interest in earnings of consolidated affiliates	29	16	13
Net earnings applicable to common stock	$ 1,409	$ 1,064	$ 986
Earnings per common share	$ 6.20	$ 4.68	$ 4.34
Share owners' equity at year end (net assets) (c)	$ 7,362	$10,436	$11,153

Use of each dollar of earnings
Based on total earnings before taxes 1975-1979

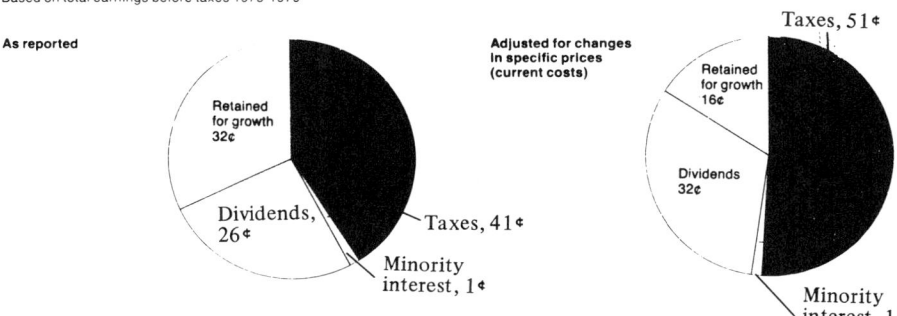

Table 2: supplementary information – effect of changing prices (a)

(In millions, except per-share amounts)

Current cost information in dollars of 1979 purchasing power (b)					
(All amounts expressed in average 1979 dollars)	1979	1978	1977	1976	1975
Sales of products and services to customers	$22,461	$21,867	$20,984	$20,015	$19,022
Cost of goods sold	16,074	15,548	14,793	14,145	13,914
Selling, general and administrative expense	3,716	3,566	3,606	3,360	3,018
Depreciation, depletion and amortization	980	1,000	986	979	1,006
Interest and other financial charges	258	249	238	222	251
Other income	(519)	(466)	(467)	(350)	(235)
Earnings before income taxes and minority interest	1,952	1,970	1,828	1,659	1,068
Provision for income taxes	953	995	926	853	620
Minority interest in earnings of consolidated affiliates	13	13	20	26	26
Net earnings applicable to common stock	$ 986	$ 962	$ 882	$ 780	$ 422
Earnings per common share	$ 4.34	$ 4.22	$ 3.88	$ 3.45	$ 1.88
Share owners' equity at year end (net assets) (c)	$11,153	$11,020	$10,656	$10,526	$10,056
Other inflation information					
Average Consumer Price Index (1967 = 100)	217.4	195.4	181.5	170.5	161.2
(Loss) gain in general purchasing power of net monetary items	$(209)	$(128)	$ (61)	$ (20)	$ 19
Dividends declared per common share	2.75	2.78	2.52	2.17	2.16
Market price per common share at year end	47⅞	50½	58¼	69⅜	60¼

General Electric Co.

Notes to supplementary information — Tables 1 and 2

(a) This information has been prepared in accordance with requirements of the Financial Accounting Standards Board (FASB). Proper use of this information requires an understanding of certain basic concepts and definitions.

The heading "As reported in the traditional statements" refers to information drawn directly from the financial statements presented on pages 32 to 44. This information is prepared using the set of generally accepted accounting principles which renders an accounting based on the number of actual dollars involved in transactions, with no recognition given to the fact that the value of the dollar changes over time.

The heading "Adjusted for general inflation" refers to information prepared using a different approach to transactions involving inventory and property, plant and equipment assets. Under this procedure, the number of dollars involved in transactions at different dates are all restated to equivalent amounts in terms of the general purchasing power of the dollar as it is measured by the Consumer Price Index for all Urban Consumers (CPI-U). For example, $1,000 invested in a building asset in 1967 would be restated to its 1979 dollar purchasing power equivalent of $2,174 to value the asset and calculate depreciation charges. Similarly, 1978 purchases of non-LIFO inventory sold in 1979 would be accounted for at their equivalent in terms of 1979 dollars, rather than in terms of the actual number of dollars spent.

The heading "Adjusted for changes in specific prices (current costs)" refers to information prepared using yet another approach to transactions involving inventory and property, plant and equipment assets. In this case, rather than restating to dollars of the same general purchasing power, estimates of current costs of the assets are used.

In presenting results of either of the supplementary accounting methods for more than one year, "real" trends are more evident when results for all years are expressed in terms of the general purchasing power of the dollar for a designated period. Results of such restatements are generally called "constant dollar" presentations. In the five-year presentations shown above, dollar results for earlier periods have been restated to their equivalent number of constant dollars of 1979 general purchasing power (CPI-U basis).

Since none of these restatements is allowable for tax purposes under existing regulations, income tax amounts are the same as in the traditional statements (but expressed in constant dollars in the five-year summary).

There are a number of other terms and concepts which may be of interest in assessing the significance of the supplementary information shown in Tables 1 and 2. However, it is management's opinion that the basic concepts discussed above are the most significant for the reader to have in mind while reviewing this information.

(b) Principal types of information used to adjust for changes in specific prices (current costs) are (1) for inventory costs, GE-generated indices of price changes for specific goods and services, and (2) for property, plant and equipment, externally generated indices of price changes for major classes of assets.

(c) At December 31, 1979, the current cost of inventory was $5,251 million, and of property, plant and equipment was $7,004 million. Estimated current costs applicable to the sum of such amounts held during all or part of 1979 increased by approximately $1,111 million, which was $329 million less than the $1,440-million increase which could be expected because of general inflation.

Exhibit 1 continued.

pact of inflation, to incorporate the perspectives provided by such measurements into decision-making, and to stimulate awareness by all levels of management of the need to develop constructive business strategies to deal with inflation. The objective is to ensure that investments needed for new business growth, productivity improvements and capacity expansions earn appropriate *real rates of return* commensurate with the risks involved. Such supplemental measurements can assist in the entire resource allocation process, starting with initial project approval, implementation and subsequent review.

Improving productivity to offset inflationary forces is a primary goal established by top management that is being stressed throughout General Electric. As discussed on the back cover of this Annual Report, the Company has committed significant levels of resources to research and development activities to accelerate innovation and increase productivity. In addition, General Electric's production base continues to be expanded and modernized through increasing investments in plant and equipment. For example, $1,262 million and $1,055 million were spent on strengthening General Electric's production base in 1979 and 1978, respectively. Imaginative and diligent coupling of production techniques and equipment is critical to the maintenance and improvement of your Company's profitability.

147

EXHIBIT 2: Shell Company
Supplementary Information Regarding Inflation and Changing Prices

For some years there has been growing concern about the impact of inflation on the performance of business enterprises as measured by traditional financial statements. In an effort to assist readers of financial statements in understanding the severity of this impact, Shell has published price-level adjusted financial information each year since 1974.

During 1979, the Financial Accounting Standards Board (FASB) issued Statement No. 33, Financial Reporting and Changing Prices, which provides new rules for the publication of certain inflation related information. The data that follows is presented in accordance with this statement. The FASB has decided, and Shell fully agrees, that traditional financial statements should be retained as the primary record of performance but that these should be supplemented by inflation adjusted information.

Shell's primary financial statements, which appear on pages 30 to 33, are prepared under generally accepted accounting principles and are known as historical cost financial statements. They record actual transactions in terms of the number of dollars received or expended without regard to changes in the purchasing power of the currency or changes in the cost of goods and services consumed. The result is that investments made over extended periods of time are added together as though the dollars involved all have the same value. Moreover, the amortization of these prior period costs is deducted from current period revenues so that net income is the result of matching revenues and costs in dollars with differing amounts of purchasing power.

Another objection to traditional financial statements is that they reflect the historic cost rather than the current cost of assets consumed. Costs change for many reasons in addition to inflation, e.g., technological improvements, changes in productivity, variations in supply and demand, etc. These changes are usually at different rates than that of general inflation. In recognition of the separate problems created by inflation and by changing prices, the FASB has mandated two forms of supplemental disclosure. One is to isolate the impact of general inflation and is called Constant Dollar reporting. The second is an attempt to identify the other components of changing prices on a company's performance as well, and is called Current Cost reporting. Both approaches are reported on page 45.

Constant Dollar Data

Constant dollar data measures the effects of general inflation on the financial results of the Company. Although some minor variations in techniques have been adopted by the FASB, in prior years we have referred to this as price-level adjusted financial information. It is calculated according to a precise mathematical procedure and is, therefore, objective and comparable among companies.

Under this method, historical cost financial information is adjusted only for changes that have occurred in the general purchasing power of the dollar as measured by the Consumer Price Index. Therefore, the result is a restatement of the traditional financial information in a common unit of measurement, which in the attached schedule is the dollar as valued at the end of 1979. It is appropriate to note that the results of this approach do not purport to represent appraised value, replacement cost, or any other measure of the current value of the underlying assets. Although the constant dollar information in this schedule is presented in summary form, comprehensive restatements were made of all financial statement elements to determine the amounts shown.

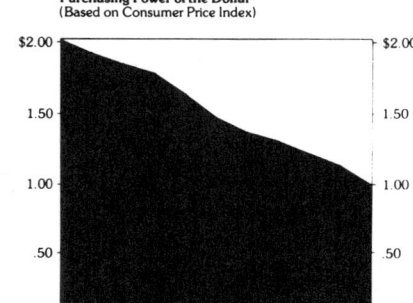

Purchasing Power of the Dollar
(Based on Consumer Price Index)

Current Cost Data

The second form of disclosure prescribed by Statement 33 measures the impact of changes in the specific prices of property, plant and equipment, inventories, depreciation and depletion, and costs and expenses.

Because of the large number of assets owned by Shell, current cost measurement of individual assets was not feasible. Therefore, various indexes were employed that appear to be compatible with the changing costs experienced by Shell. Although the resulting estimates are believed to be reasonable, they do involve a number of subjective judgments. For example, about one-fourth of the balance in the property, plant and equipment categories is for unexpired costs of developing oil and gas reserves. The current cost adjustment was made by applying an index based on the industry's average cost of drilling and equipping wells. Therefore, the results are not projections of future costs but are approximations of the amounts that would result had past drilling and development occurred at today's prices. The adjusted amounts for depreciation, depletion and amortization are based on these same premises. All current costs are expressed in year-end 1979 dollars.

Purchasing Power Gain on Net Monetary Items

In addition to the impacts just described, inflation also affects monetary assets and liabilities. Holders of cash and receivables lose purchasing power during inflationary periods because they will buy less as prices rise. Conversely, those holding liabilities stand to gain because less purchas-

Exhibit 2 continued.   Shell Company

Historical Dollars 1979	Millions of dollars, except per share amounts	Dollars of Current Purchasing Power*			
		Constant Dollar Data		Current Cost Data	
		1979	1978	1979	1978
	Summary Statement of Income				
$14,546	Revenues	$15,374	$13,081	$15,374	$13,081
	Cost and Expenses:				
704	Depreciation, depletion, etc.	1,107	1,015	1,219	1,217
1,090	Income and operating taxes	1,152	917	1,152	917
11,626	Other costs and expenses	12,337	10,545	12,362	10,684
1,126	Income from Continuing Operations	778	604	$ 641	$ 263
	Purchasing power gain on net monetary items	337	236	$ 337	$ 236
$ 1,126	Net Income	$ 1,115	$ 840		
	Increase in current cost valuation of inventory and property, plant & equipment held during year			$ 2,149	$ 1,158
	Effect of increases in general price level			1,754	1,176
	Excess of increase in specific prices over increase in general price level................			$ 395	$ (18)
	Balance Sheet Data				
$ 520	Inventories of Oils and Chemicals	$ 880	$ 890	$ 2,231	$ 1,557
$12,385	Net Property, Plant & Equipment	$16,043	$11,469	$17,178	$13,051
$ 7,004	Shareholders' Equity	$11,131	$10,257	$13,617	$12,505
	Per Share Data†				
$ 7.32	Income from Continuing Operations	$ 5.06	$ 4.05	$ 4.17	$ 1.76
$ 7.32	Net Income	$ 7.26	$ 5.63	—	—

Five-Year Comparisons (In December 1979 dollars)	1979	1978	1977	1976	1975
Revenues..	$15,374	$13,081	$12,912	$12,551	$11,732
Constant dollar net income	$ 1,115	$ 840	$ 805	$ 778	$ 593
Cash dividends per share†	$ 2.22	$ 2.04	$ 1.98	$ 1.85	$ 1.80
Closing market price per share	$ 54.25	$ 36.54	$ 41.37	$ 52.02	$ 33.86
Consumer price index — end of year	229.9	202.9	186.1	174.3	166.3
Ratios:					
Net Income to Shareholders' Equity:					
Historical cost basis	18.4%	15.1%	16.2%	18.2%	14.4%
Constant dollar basis..........................	10.9%	8.8%	9.1%	9.7%	7.7%
Income from Continuing Operations to Shareholders' Equity:					
Historical cost basis	18.4%	15.1%	16.2%	18.2%	14.4%
Constant dollar basis........................	7.6%	6.3%	7.4%	8.5%	6.0%
Current cost basis	5.1%	2.2%	—	—	—

*Current cost and constant dollar amounts are expressed in December 1979 dollars. Changes are measured by the consumer price index.

†Per weighted average shares outstanding each year.

Shell Company

ing power will be required to satisfy their obligations. These gains and losses have long been considered to be an integral part of the constant dollar concept of income and are therefore included in constant dollar "Net Income" in the table on page 45.

Income Taxes

In conformance with Statement 33, income taxes included in the supplemental statement of income are the same as reported in the primary financial statements except that the amounts are expressed in year-end dollars. Present tax laws do not allow deductions for higher depreciation or other cost adjustments for the effects of inflation. Consequently, taxes are levied on industry and individuals at effective rates well in excess of statutory rates for many years following periods of high inflation.

Review of Information Presented

As shown on page 46, Shell has reported substantial growth in both sales and net income under traditional accounting measurements. A further perspective of Shell's progress is obtained by expressing all financial statement amounts in constant dollars. On this basis, Income from Continuing Operations was $778 million in 1979, significantly lower than the comparable historic cost measurement. The high rates of inflation also caused large purchasing power gains on Shell's net monetary liabilities. When these gains are added to Income from Continuing Operations the resulting Net Income is about the same as historic cost Net Income. However, it is important to relate any measure of income to the investment required to generate it. As indicated in the Five-Year Comparisons on page 45, Shell's profitability ratios are significantly lower when both income and Shareholders' Equity are stated in constant dollars. For example, the 1979 ratio of Net Income to Shareholders' Equity is reduced from 18.4 percent to 10.9 percent when viewed on a constant dollar basis.

Although current cost data is of necessity subjective, it provides an approximation of the margin between Shell's current revenues and the current costs of goods consumed and services utilized. During 1979 and 1978, this margin was substantially less than income based on historical costs.

In addition, Statement 33 requires that current cost disclosures include supplemental information on changes in the purchasing power of monetary items and changes in the current cost of inventories and property, plant and equipment. The FASB believes these disclosures may provide information that is useful as an indicator of potential future cash flows.

Shell's 1979 increase in the current cost of inventories and property, plant and equipment was largely attributable to the rising costs of crude oil and increasing costs of productive facilities. Shell believes it is important to recognize that such increases would only be realized in the unlikely event that these assets were totally liquidated.

---

to nonmonetary assets. Several public enterprises have significant investments in nonmonetary assets such as equity subsidiaries and joint ventures, intangible assets (patents), and marketable securities. These assets are affected by inflation but Statement No. 33 does not require their adjustments. With flexibility accorded to these public enterprises, some have adjusted these assets while others have not, which have led to confusion and incomplete and noncomparable data. The five-year disclosure of net assets has also been affected by the different treatment accorded to nonmonetary assets, especially when they are material in amount.

Similarly, a comprehensive restatement would require unconsolidated finance subsidiaries to be restated for the impact of inflation (note that Statement No. 33 does not require unconsolidated finance subsidiaries and other equity investments to be restated). Since substantially all the assets and liabilities of a finance subsidiary are monetary, a monetary loss will result to the extent of the parent company's equity investment during a period of inflation. By substituting a nonmonetary investment that is not adjusted for inflation for the subsidiary's monetary assets, the parent company can show different results than if the subsidiaries were consolidated.

Another shortcoming is the requirement to use average-for-the-year dollars rather than the end-of-the-year dollars. The use of the average-for-the-year dollars to simplify calculation and avoid adjustments to revenue and certain other expenses has led to year-end inventories, market price of stocks and dividends being reported at lower absolute amounts than historical cost when they are adjusted to constant dollars using average-for-the-year dollars. It could be difficult to explain to the layman why inventory, market price of stocks and dividends adjusted for the effects of inflation are deflated while property, plant and equipment are inflated.

The option given by Statement No. 33 that allows the five-year summary of constant dollar information to be presented in terms of a base year that can either be the current year or the base year of the Consumer Price Index (1967) has led to unnecessary confusion. The use of the current year dollar as the base year would require the five-year summary information to be restated every year. This restatement every year would change the previous four years' information which will add to further confusion. Nevertheless, users of supplementary information who want to make company-to-company comparison should watch for such differences. The conversion of a company's data from one base year to the base year (which is different) of the other company is not difficult since the index for each year is provided. To convert, multiply the data by a fraction, the numerator of which is the index for the base year you want the data in and the denominator of which is the index for the base year the data are in.

The exclusion of the purchasing power gain or loss from the determination of constant-dollar income would seem to raise some doubt as to whether such gains or losses are real. The purchasing power gain or loss is a real reflection of inflation and the requirement that it be reported separately makes the constant-dollar statements more difficult to explain.

These are some problems that arose from the early application of the Statement and represent deficiencies which present problems in quality and comparability of the information. Despite these deficiencies, some trends and patterns are emerging from the information being reported.

One leading accountant has made the following observations based on emerging trends and patterns.[1]

1. *Income from operations, excluding purchasing power gain or loss, will decrease.* The extent of the decrease will depend on the industry, but overall the decrease will probably exceed 40%. The major cause of the decrease is price-level-adjusted depreciation expense. A secondary cause is the effect of holding inventories during a time of inflation. For example, General Electric, General Motors and Shell Oil reported decreases from historical-cost income to constant-dollar income of 24%, 39% and 31%. Their current-cost decreases were similar. These companies are all on LIFO. If they were on FIFO, the declines would have been more significant. More capital-intensive companies, such as Inland Steel and American Telephone and Telegraph, had larger decreases—53% and 70%. Historical cost captures such inflation gains in inventory leading to the so-called inflationary profits. These profits are eliminated from constant-dollar disclosures.

2. *Tax rates will skyrocket.* On an average, they may increase by as much as 25% to an effective rate of 55% to 65%. This was the increase in the effective tax rate in a 1974 survey of 80 companies on the impact of constant-dollar accounting. In 1979, General Electric, General Motors and Shell Oil had increases in effective tax rates of 7% (from 40% to 47%), 13% (from 45% to 58%) and 7% (from 46% to 53%). Many utilities' tax rates are close to 100% on an adjusted basis. Many companies are prominently displaying such tax rates to emphasize the need for legislation.

3. *The purchasing power gain or loss will vary significantly from company to company.* By and large, it will be a gain. In fact,

---

[1] *Inflation and Its Impact on Financial Executives* by Duane R. Kullberg, Chairman and Chief Executive Officer, Arthur Andersen and Company, May 30, 1980.

for the average company the purchasing power gain may just about equal the decrease in operating income resulting from adjusting depreciation and inventory, plant and equipment. Thus, the fact that Statement 33 does not include the purchasing power gain in restated income will tend to exaggerate the negative impact of inflation. Some conservatively capitalized companies such as IBM, however, show a loss from monetary items.

4. *Rates of return on stockholders' equity will decline.* Return on investment decreases dramatically as a result of both the decline in earnings and the increase in equity resulting from price-level adjustments to inventory and property, plant and equipment.

5. *Debt-to-equity ratios will improve.* A potential benefit of constant-dollar adjustments could be a more realistic assessment of debt-to-equity ratios. Such ratios have deteriorated in historical dollars. However, rules of thumb for financial analysis purposes have not changed. If the improvement resulting from inflation adjustments is widely accepted, some of the pressure for off-balance-sheet financing may be mitigated. Ultimately, the importance of Statement 33 will be measured by the reaction of the investment community. Investment analysts are already making some interesting observations on the impact of constant-dollar accounting.

6. *Many companies are reporting deflated or decreasing dividend rates.* Those companies whose dividend increases have fallen below the rate of general price inflation may be encouraged to increase their dividends. However, dividend payout ratios may be used to defend against raising dividends. For example, in constant dollars, General Motors had a dividend payout ratio of 86% (compared to 53% in historical dollars), Inland Steel of 97% compared to 45%, and American Telephone and Telegraph of 204% compared to 62%.

7. *Resistance to LIFO may decrease.* Some companies have resisted the use of LIFO because of its negative impact on nominal dollar earnings. Such resistance may decrease since constant-dollar costs of sales approximate LIFO cost of sales. The tax

advantages of LIFO are more likely to overcome the perceived accounting result disadvantages of LIFO.

8. *New tests for evaluating leverage barriers or debt-equity ratios may emerge.* Some companies with weak debt-equity ratios in nominal terms will be perceived to be stronger than expected in constant terms. Maybe there will be a return to the more traditional forms of financing.

9. *Pricing policies may be reconsidered.* Restated expense information is revealing that on a constant-dollar basis, price increases may not be keeping up with inflation in certain industries. All of this suggests a need for a real sensitivity to the effects of inflation on operating and financing decisions.

Traditional management rules to manage a public enterprise do not change during a period of inflation. Inflation, however, results in additional emphasis being placed on certain rules. The following is a list of positive things a public enterprise (and mostly everyone else) can do to increase return during a time of inflation:[2]

1. *Minimize monetary assets.* Companies' treasurers have grown quite sophisticated in this area, and perhaps there is no room for improvement in such things as cash collections, the use of lock box systems and the timely investment of available cash. However, accounts receivable are also monetary assets. Some companies carry receivables as part of a marketing strategy. This strategy should be evaluated in light of inflation.

2. *Review credit and collection policies.* Credit limits, payment terms, deposit requirements, progress payments, discount availability and collection procedures require special consideration in times of inflation, as do policies regarding delinquent accounts. It may no longer be profitable to carry the customers' receivables for 90 days or more. That kind of marginal business may not be profitable during times of inflation.

3. *Maximize monetary liabilities.* This is the one management rule that differs under inflation from traditional corporate fi-

[2] *Ibid.*

nancial management. Everyone understands the advantages of being in debt during times of inflation. An article in the March 12 edition of *The Wall Street Journal* suggested that inflation has helped reduce bankruptcy because borrowings are paid back in cheaper dollars. The Journal pointed out that the bankruptcy rate in 1961 was 64 out of every 10,000 companies that went under. In 1979, the rate had dropped to 30 out of every 10,000. Price-level information will be helpful when seeking funds to borrow. Restated debt-equity ratios will also be helpful in selling the company's financial strength. Debt provides a hedge during times of inflation. Obviously, the benefits of the hedge must be weighed against the risks of further leveraging and the interest rate on the debt.

4. *Manage nonmonetary assets.* Inventory is a particularly important asset to manage during inflationary times. Product pricing is critical. It is essential that companies review inventory systems to make certain that management receives needed information on a timely basis. Inventory systems must provide current-cost information continuously to provide the information necessary for proper product pricing. Decisions to increase prices must be made quickly and accurately. Obviously, escalation clauses should be incorporated into pricing whenever possible. Inventory levels are important in inflation, and inflation itself becomes an important element of inventory carrying costs. Inventory carrying costs should be recalculated because inflation is a negative carrying cost. Inventory may be a better investment than marketable securities if prices in your industry are rising faster than general price changes. But if specific prices in the industry lag general price increases, then inventory should be minimized and the resulting cash flow should be invested in marketable securities. It is obvious that the impact of inflation on inventories is different from that of receivables.

5. *Plan in inflation-adjusted dollars.* Inflation's impact on the business should be more important to internal management than to stockholders. Projections and business plans should utilize inflation-adjusted data, and several assumptions about levels of inflation may be used to achieve flexibility. Computerized financial modeling may be helpful to provide timely adjustments in a period of rapidly changing prices. It will be

necessary for management to face up to the company's actual performance on an inflation-adjusted basis. If management doesn't, the market certainly will. Planning based on inflation is not new to some companies. Shell Oil, for example, uses inflation-adjusted data in internal reports, and General Electric does its planning in current-cost dollars. In its annual report, General Electric points out that its objective "is to ensure that investments needed for new business growth, productivity improvements and capacity expansions earn appropriate real rates of return commensurate with the risks involved."

6. *Reevaluate tax-planning decisions.* Decisions that were rejected in the past because of marginal benefits may now have a positive impact on earnings because of inflation. Because taxes are paid on both real profits and inflation profits, the tax system really confiscates capital. As a result, it may be necessary to reconsider adopting LIFO. Depreciation lives and methods should be reconsidered so maximum amounts are claimed. Receivable reserves should reflect collection slowdowns. Pension payments should be delayed as long as the law permits.

7. *Capital needs must be carefully planned and evaluated in relation to capital availability.* Leasing should be considered as an additional source of funds. Sale and leaseback transactions may free up funds. Factoring receivables may provide a source of cash. Joint-venture arrangements are becoming a more popular vehicle for financing large projects. Dividend policies may also need reconsideration. Each of these possibilities involves good, common sense management.

SUMMARY

Traditional financial statements have been prepared based mainly on historical costs, with the use of a variety of current value measurements. In order for financial reporting to provide meaningful and useful financial information to internal and external decision makers, financial reporting has to adjust itself to the changing economic, legal, political and social environment. With inflation running above 10 percent, traditional accounting data often presents false comfort.

Inflation adjusted data may provide more meaningful and useful information for management decision making.

FASB Statement No. 33 establishes standards of reporting for both general inflation and changes in specific prices. It applies to public corporations having total assets of $1 billion or more after deducting depreciation or having inventories plus gross property, plant and equipment of $125 million or more. The Statement requires no change in the basic financial statement and the required information is to be presented in supplementary statements, schedules or supplementary notes in the financial reports.

Although several problems have been detected in applying Statement No. 33, trends and patterns have emerged from the information reported that will prove useful to the various decision makers. This information will enable the management of the corporation to emphasize certain management rules in managing the corporation to maximize returns during a period of inflation.

Appendix

APPENDIX A

U. S. Department of Labor, Consumer Price Index for All Urban Consumers (CPI-U) (1967=100)

Year	Jan.	Feb.	Mar.	Apr.	May	June	July	Aug.	Sep.	Oct.	Nov.	Dec.	Avg.
1919	49.5	48.4	49.0	49.9	50.6	50.7	52.1	53.0	53.3	54.2	55.5	56.7	51.8
1920	57.8	58.5	59.1	60.8	61.8	62.7	62.3	60.7	60.0	59.7	59.3	58.0	60.0
1921	57.0	55.2	54.8	54.1	53.1	52.8	52.9	53.1	52.5	52.4	52.1	51.8	53.6
1922	50.7	50.6	50.0	50.0	50.0	50.1	50.2	49.7	49.8	50.1	50.3	50.5	50.2
1923	50.3	50.2	50.4	50.6	50.7	51.0	51.5	51.3	51.6	51.7	51.8	51.8	51.1
1924	51.7	51.5	51.2	51.0	51.0	51.0	51.1	51.0	51.2	51.4	51.6	51.7	51.2
1925	51.8	51.6	51.7	51.6	51.8	52.4	53.1	53.1	52.9	53.1	54.0	53.7	52.5
1926	53.7	53.5	53.2	53.7	53.4	53.0	52.5	52.2	52.5	52.7	52.9	52.9	53.0
1927	52.5	52.1	51.8	51.8	52.2	52.7	51.7	51.4	51.7	52.0	51.9	51.8	52.0
1928	51.7	51.2	51.2	51.3	51.6	51.2	51.2	51.3	51.7	51.6	51.5	51.3	51.3
1929	51.2	51.1	50.9	50.7	51.0	51.2	51.7	51.9	51.8	51.8	51.7	51.4	51.3
1930	51.2	51.0	50.7	51.0	50.7	50.4	49.7	49.4	49.7	49.4	49.0	48.3	50.0
1931	47.6	46.9	46.6	46.3	45.8	45.3	45.2	45.1	44.9	44.6	44.1	43.7	45.6
1932	42.8	42.2	42.0	41.7	41.1	40.8	40.8	40.3	40.1	39.8	39.6	39.2	40.9
1933	38.6	38.0	37.7	37.6	37.7	38.1	39.2	39.6	39.6	39.6	39.6	39.4	38.8
1934	39.6	39.9	39.9	39.8	39.9	40.0	40.0	40.1	40.7	40.4	40.3	40.2	40.1
1935	40.8	41.1	41.0	41.4	41.2	41.1	40.9	40.9	41.1	41.1	41.3	41.4	41.1
1936	41.4	41.2	41.0	41.0	41.0	41.4	41.6	41.9	42.0	41.9	41.9	41.9	41.5
1937	42.2	42.3	42.6	42.8	43.0	43.1	43.3	43.4	43.8	43.6	43.3	43.2	43.0
1938	42.6	42.2	42.2	42.4	42.2	42.2	42.3	42.2	42.2	42.0	41.9	42.0	42.2
1939	41.8	41.6	41.5	41.4	41.4	41.4	41.4	41.4	42.2	42.0	42.0	41.8	41.6
1940	41.7	42.0	41.9	41.9	42.0	42.1	42.0	41.9	42.0	42.0	42.0	42.2	42.0
1941	42.2	42.2	42.4	42.8	43.1	43.9	44.1	44.5	45.3	45.8	46.2	46.3	44.1
1942	46.9	47.3	47.9	48.2	48.7	48.8	49.0	49.3	49.4	49.9	50.2	50.6	48.8
1943	50.6	50.7	51.5	52.1	52.5	52.4	52.0	51.8	52.0	52.2	52.1	52.2	51.8
1944	52.1	52.0	52.0	52.3	52.5	52.6	52.9	53.1	53.1	53.1	53.1	53.3	52.7
1945	53.3	53.2	53.2	53.3	53.7	54.2	54.3	54.3	54.1	54.1	54.3	54.5	53.9

159

Year	1	2	3	4	5	6	7	8	9	10	11	12	13
1946	54.5	54.3	54.7	55.0	55.3	55.9	59.2	60.5	61.2	62.4	63.9	64.4	58.5
1947	64.4	64.3	65.2	65.7	65.5	66.0	66.6	67.3	68.9	68.9	69.3	70.2	66.9
1948	71.0	70.4	70.2	71.2	71.7	72.2	73.1	73.2	73.4	73.1	72.6	72.1	72.1
1949	72.0	71.2	71.4	71.5	71.4	71.5	71.0	71.2	71.5	71.1	71.2	70.8	71.4
1950	70.5	70.3	70.6	70.7	71.0	71.4	72.1	72.7	73.2	73.6	73.9	74.9	72.1
1951	76.1	77.0	77.3	77.4	77.7	77.6	77.7	77.7	78.2	78.6	79.0	79.3	77.8
1952	79.3	78.3	78.8	79.1	79.2	79.4	80.0	80.1	80.0	80.1	80.1	80.0	79.5
1953	79.8	79.4	79.6	79.7	79.9	80.2	80.4	80.6	80.7	80.9	80.6	80.5	80.1
1954	80.7	80.6	80.5	80.3	80.6	80.7	80.7	80.6	80.4	80.2	80.3	80.1	80.5
1955	80.1	80.1	80.1	80.1	80.1	80.1	80.4	80.2	80.5	80.5	80.6	80.4	80.2
1956	80.3	80.3	80.4	80.5	89.9	81.4	82.0	81.9	82.0	82.5	82.5	82.7	81.4
1957	82.8	83.1	83.3	83.6	83.8	84.3	84.7	84.8	84.9	84.9	85.2	85.2	84.3
1958	85.7	85.8	86.4	86.6	86.6	86.7	86.8	86.7	86.7	86.7	86.8	86.7	86.6
1959	86.8	86.7	86.7	86.8	86.9	87.3	87.5	87.4	87.7	88.0	88.0	88.0	87.3
1960	87.9	88.0	88.0	88.5	88.5	88.7	88.7	88.7	88.8	89.2	89.3	89.3	88.7
1961	89.3	89.3	89.3	89.3	89.3	89.4	89.8	89.7	89.9	89.9	89.9	89.9	89.6
1962	89.9	90.1	90.3	90.5	90.5	90.5	90.7	90.7	91.2	91.1	91.1	91.0	90.6
1963	91.1	91.2	91.3	91.3	91.3	91.7	92.1	92.1	92.1	92.2	92.3	92.5	91.7
1964	92.6	92.5	92.6	92.7	92.7	92.9	93.1	93.0	93.2	93.3	93.5	93.6	92.9
1965	93.6	93.6	93.7	94.0	94.2	94.7	94.8	94.6	94.8	94.9	95.1	95.4	94.5
1966	95.4	96.0	96.3	96.7	96.8	97.1	97.4	97.9	98.1	98.5	98.5	98.6	97.2
1967	98.6	98.7	98.9	99.1	99.4	99.7	100.2	100.5	100.7	101.0	101.3	101.6	100.0
1968	102.0	102.3	102.8	103.1	103.4	104.0	104.5	104.8	105.1	105.7	106.1	106.4	104.2
1969	106.7	107.1	108.0	108.7	109.0	109.7	110.2	110.7	111.2	111.6	112.2	112.9	109.8
1970	113.3	113.9	114.5	115.2	115.7	116.3	116.7	116.9	117.5	118.1	118.5	119.1	116.3
1971	119.2	119.4	119.8	120.2	120.8	121.5	121.8	122.1	122.2	122.4	122.6	123.1	121.3
1972	123.2	123.8	124.0	124.8	124.7	125.0	125.5	125.7	126.2	126.6	126.9	127.3	125.3
1973	127.7	128.6	129.8	130.7	131.5	132.4	132.7	135.1	135.5	136.6	137.6	138.5	133.1
1974	139.7	141.5	143.1	143.9	145.5	146.9	148.0	149.9	151.7	153.0	154.3	155.4	147.7
1975	156.1	157.2	157.8	158.6	159.3	160.6	162.3	162.8	163.6	164.6	165.6	166.3	161.2
1976	166.7	167.1	167.5	168.2	169.2	170.1	171.1	171.9	172.6	173.3	173.8	174.3	170.5
1977	175.3	177.1	178.2	179.6	180.6	181.8	182.6	183.3	184.0	184.5	185.4	186.1	181.5
1978	187.2	188.4	189.8	191.5	193.3	195.3	196.7	197.8	199.3	200.9	202.0	202.9	195.4
1979	204.7	207.1	209.1	211.5	214.1	216.6	218.9	221.1	223.4	225.4	227.5	229.9	217.4

Appendix

GLOSSARY

Accelerated Depreciation. A generally accepted depreciation method that results in progressively smaller amounts of depreciation expense each accounting period until the total depreciable cost of a long-lived asset has been expensed. Examples are: sum-of-the-years' digits method and the double-declining-balance method.

Account. A device used for recording increases and decreases in specific assets, liabilities, and components of owners' equity. In its simplest form, an account resembles the letter "T". Every account consists of an account title, an account number, and a left and right side.

Account Payable. A liability representing an amount due to a creditor, usually in payment for purchases of merchandise, materials, or supplies.

Account Receivable. An asset representing an amount owed to a business by a customer, usually arising from the sale of merchandise or services.

Accounting. The process of identifying, measuring, and communicating economic information to permit informed judgments and decisions by users of the information. Accounting is a service activity that provides financial information about an entity that is useful in making rational investment, credit, and similar decisions.

Accounting Concepts. Broad fundamental concepts that have helped provide a basis for the establishment of generally accepted accounting principles.

Accounting Cycle. Another name for the *accounting process*.

Accounting Equation. Assets equal liabilities plus owners' equity. (A = L + OE)

Accounting Period. A period of time at the end of which the basic financial statements are prepared. Commonly used accounting periods are a month, three months, six months, nine months, and a year.

Accounting Policies. The specific accounting principles and practices adopted by a business.

Accounting Principles. Those concepts, methods, and procedures that have become generally accepted as the basis for recording business transactions and for the preparation of an enterprise's financial statements.

Accrual Basis of Accounting. A method of income determination whereby revenues are recorded at the time they are earned and expenses are recorded at the time they are incurred.

Accumulated Depreciation. A contra-asset account that is subtracted from a long-lived asset for purposes of balance sheet presentation. The balance in the accumulated depreciation account represents the sum of the depreciation expense recorded relative to the long-lived asset to date. The original cost of a long-lived asset minus the accumulated depreciation on that asset results in an amount referred to as the book value of the long-lived asset.

Adjunct Account. An account whose balance is added to the balance of another account for purposes of balance sheet presentation. The account *premium on bonds payable* is an example of an adjunct account.

Allowance for Uncollectible Accounts. A contra-account to accounts receivable that represents the estimated amount of accounts receivable that an enterprise expects not to be able to collect.

Annual Report. The report prepared for a company's stockholders and other interested parties that a company prepares annually following the end of the fiscal year. It frequently includes a letter to the shareholders from the Chairman of the Board, management's discussion of previous financial performance, and a variety of financial highlights in addition to the basic financial statements. The annual report also includes the auditor's report wherein the independent accountants express an opinion as to the fairness of the financial data presented in the financial statements.

Glossary

Appropriated Retained Earnings. Retained earnings that have been earmarked for a specific purpose and consequently cannot be used as the basis for paying a dividend.

Asset. Something of value owned by a business entity. An asset may be tangible or intangible.

Audit. A comprehensive review and evaluation of an enterprise's accounting records for the purpose of expressing an opinion on the financial statements prepared from those records. Audits are performed by independent certified public accountants.

Auditor's Report. A statement made by an independent certified public accounting firm, wherein the firm expresses its opinion, using somewhat standardized terminology, that: (1) the accounting firm has examined and tested the records upon which a company's financial statements were prepared, and (2) in the accounting firm's opinion, the financial statements fairly present the financial position, changes in the financial position, and results of operations for the company in conformity with generally accepted accounting principles applied on a basis consistent with that of the previous year.

Bad Debt. An account receivable considered to be uncollectible.

Bad Debt Expense. An estimate (if the allowance method is used) of the dollar amount of credit sales made during the accounting period that will eventually prove to be uncollectible. The actual bad debts that are written-off if the direct write-off method is used.

Balance. The difference between the total left hand entries and the total right hand entries made in an account.

Balance Sheet. A financial statement showing that an enterprise's total assets are equal to its total liabilities plus owners' equity. The account form of the balance sheet shows assets on the left side and liabilities and owners' equity on the right side. The report form of the balance sheet shows assets listed first then liabilities and owners' equity listed below the assets. The balance sheet is also called the *statement of financial position.*

Bond. A debt certificate. The principal amount to be repaid upon maturity is referred to as the par value or the face value of the bond. The bond coupon rate is the annual rate of interest payable in accordance with the terms of the bond issue. Bonds frequently are issued in $1,000 units and pay interest semi-annually.

Bond Discount. The amount by which the net proceeds of a bond issue are less than the amount of the principal that must be repaid at maturity. The amount of the bond discount must be amortized over the life of the bond issue, the effect of which is to make the bond's effective rate of interest greater than its coupon rate of interest.

Bond Indenture. The written contract between the issuer of bonds and the bond holders, wherein the details associated with the bond issue are specified.

Bond Premium. The amount by which the net proceeds of a bond issue exceed the amount of the bond principal that must be repaid upon maturity. The amount of the bond premium must be amortized over the life of the bond issue, the effect of which is to make the bond's effective rate of interest less than its coupon rate of interest.

Book Value. The amount shown in an organization's books for any asset, liability, or owners' equity account. The book value of a depreciable asset is its original cost less its accumulated depreciation. The book value of an organization is the excess of its total assets over total liabilities. The book value per share of common stock is a company's stockholders' equity divided by the number of shares of common stock outstanding.

Business Combination. When a corporation and one or more incorporated or unincorporated businesses are brought together into one accounting entity, but not necessarily into one legal entity.

Capital. Another name for owners' equity. Also used to mean the total assets of an organization.

Capital Budgeting. The process of selecting from among a variety of investment proposals for the acquisition of long-lived assets. This process frequently considers the present value of projected cash flows for proposed investments. It may also include consideration of the alternative means of financing future capital investments.

Capital Stock. Equity securities of a corporation representing ownership. Capital stock consists of both common stock and preferred stock.

Capital Surplus. Another name for capital in excess of par (or stated) value of common stock. Use of this term has been discouraged in recent years.

Capital in Excess of Par Value. Represents the amount paid into a corporation in exchange for its capital stock in excess of the par value of the capital stock issued.

Cash Basis of Accounting. A method of accounting whereby revenues are recorded at the time the cash is received and expenses are recorded at the time cash disbursements are made. Unlike the accrual basis of accounting, no attempt is made to match revenues with the expenses incurred in generating those revenues.

Cash Discount. A reduction in an item's sale price granted whenever payment is made within a specified period of time.

Cash Flow Statement. A statement of changes in financial position that explains what caused the change in a company's cash balance during a specified period of time. Also, a statement of cash receipts and cash disbursements.

Certified Public Accountant (CPA). An accountant who has passed the Uniform CPA examination prepared by the American Institute of CPAs and who has met the prescribed educational, experience, and other requirements of the state issuing the CPA certificate.

Chart of Accounts. An organized listing of the names and corresponding numbers of the accounts in an organization's ledger.

Collateral. Specific assets pledged by a borrower to a lender as part of a loan agreement. These assets may be claimed by the lender if the borrower is not able to repay the loan.

Common Stock. Capital stock that does not carry any preference with regard to dividends or to distribution of assets in the case of liquidation. Common stock usually carries the right to vote at the annual stockholders' meeting, and common stockholders are the "true" owners of a corporation.

Compensating Balances. The percent of a line of credit or of a loan that a bank requires a borrower to keep on deposit at the bank. The amount of the compensating balance is negotiated between the bank and the borrower, and the effect of the compensating balance is to increase the effective interest rate of any amount borrowed.

Compound Interest. A method of calculating interest whereby interest is figured both on the principal of a loan plus any interest previously earned but not distributed.

Conservatism. An accounting concept that states: provide for all possible losses but do not record any gains or profits until they are actually realized.

Consolidated Financial Statements. Financial statements prepared for a business entity composed of a number of separate legal corporations operated as one business organization. They are prepared based on the financial statements of the individual companies, but all inter-company assets, liabilities, equities, revenues, and expenses must be eliminated.

Contra-Account. An account whose balance is subtracted from the balance of another account. Accumulated depreciation and discount on bonds payable are two examples of contra-accounts.

Contributed Capital. The sum of the capital stock accounts and the capital in excess of par (or stated) value accounts. Also called paid-in capital.

Convertible Bond. A bond whose terms of issuance gives the bond holder the right to convert the bond to a specified number of shares of capital stock during a specified future period of time.

Convertible Preferred Stock. Preferred stock whose terms of issuance give the preferred stockholders the right to convert their stock into a specified number of shares of common stock during a specified future period of time.

Corporation. A legal entity whose charter is granted according to state law.

Cost of Goods Manufactured. The total cost associated with a manufactured product. Included in this cost are materials, labor, and manufacturing overhead.

Cost of Goods Sold. The cost associated with the goods that were sold by an enterprise during a specified period of time.

Current Assets. Cash and other assets that normally will be converted into cash or used within a year or within an operating cycle of a particular business, whichever is longer. Current assets include cash, marketable securities, accounts receivable, inventory, and current prepayments.

Current Cost Accounting. A method of accounting based on current costs rather than on historical costs. Certain current cost data are required to be disclosed as supplementary information by FASB Statement No. 33.

Current Liabilities. A liability whose repayment will require the use of a current asset. As a practical matter, current liabilities may be thought of as those that are due within one year of the balance sheet date. Current liabilities include accounts payable, short-term notes payable, and other types of short-term liabilities.

Debenture. An unsecured bond.

Glossary

Deferred Charge. An asset that represents an expenditure whose related expense will not be recognized in the financial statements until a future period. At such time, the deferred charge will be written off the books and an expense will be recognized. Prepaid rent is an example of a deferred charge.

Deferred Credit. A seldom used term that represents an unusual type of liability. Customer deposits are frequently thought of as deferred credits.

Deferred Income Tax Liability. A liability that represents the accumulated difference between the income tax expense reported on a company's books and the lesser income tax actually incurred by the company. This difference arises because of significant differences in the way a company reports various revenue and expense items on its books and the way it reports these same items on its tax return. For example, a company may report depreciation on a straight-line basis for external reporting purposes but on an accelerated basis for income tax purposes.

Depletion. A non-cash expense similar to depreciation but incurred by using-up a natural resource.

Depreciation. A non-cash expense representing a portion of a company's investment (cost) in long-lived assets allocated to a particular accounting period. In calculating depreciation, it is necessary to estimate the useful lives of the long-lived assets and to estimate salvage values at the end of their useful lives. Depreciation may be thought of as the process of allocating the cost of a long-lived asset, less any estimated salvage value, over its estimated useful life in a systematic and rational manner. Depreciation is a process of allocation, not a process of valuation.

Dividend. A distribution of earnings to the stockholders of a corporation, usually in the form of cash.

Donated Capital. The increase in owners' equity resulting from a donation of an asset to a company. Generally recorded at fair market value.

Double-Declining-Balance Depreciation. A method of calculating depreciation whereby a percentage equal to twice the straight-line percentage is multiplied by the declining book value to determine the depreciation expense for the period. Salvage value is ignored when calculating double-declining-balance depreciation.

Double-Entry Accounting. A system of accounting that requires the financial consequences of every transaction be recorded by equal amounts placed on the left side of some accounts and on the right side of other accounts.

Thus, every transaction results in the recording of equal left-hand and right-hand amounts.

Double Taxation. When after-tax income is distributed to shareholders in the form of dividends and such dividends are again taxed as income to the stockholders.

Doubtful Account. An account receivable thought to be uncollectible.

Earned Surplus. Another name for retained earnings. Use of this term has been discouraged in recent years.

Earnings. Income or profit.

Effective Interest Rate. The true interest rate incurred by a borrower. The effective interest rate of a bond is frequently referred to as the *yield to maturity* at the time of the bond issue.

Equities. Liabilities plus owners' equity.

Expense. The decrease in owners' equity (net assets) incurred during an accounting period for the purpose of earning revenue.

External Reporting. Financial reporting to stockholders and others outside of an enterprise.

Extraordinary Items. Items affecting net income that are both unusual in nature and infrequent in their occurrence compared with the typical or normal activities of a business entity. When extraordinary items occur, the income statement should show (a) income before extraordinary items, (b) extraordinary items, and (c) net income.

Face Amount of a Bond. The par value, stated value, or maturity value of a bond.

Factory Overhead. Another name for manufacturing overhead.

Federal Income Tax. The income tax levied by the federal government on corporations and individuals.

Financial Accounting. Provides external users with quantitative information regarding an enterprise's economic resources, obligations, and financial performance.

Financial Statement. The four basic financial statements are: the balance sheet,

Glossary

the income statement, the statement of retained earnings, and the statement of changes in financial position.

Finished Goods Inventory. Completed inventory that is ready to be sold.

First-In, First-Out (FIFO). The inventory costing method by which the cost of ending inventory is determined from the cost of the most recent purchases and cost of goods sold is determined from the cost associated with the oldest purchases, including beginning inventory.

Fiscal Year. The twelve-month (or 52-53 week) period selected by a business as its accounting period for financial reporting purposes. It may or may not be a calendar year.

Fixed Assets. Long-lived assets acquired to be used in the business rather than to be sold. Fixed assets may be both tangible and intangible.

FOB. Free-on-Board, some location. Examples are FOB Shipping Point and FOB Destination. The location denotes the point at which title passes from the seller to the buyer.

Footnotes. Informative disclosures appended to and considered to be a part of a company's published financial statements. Footnotes frequently cover such matters as basis of consolidation, depreciation and inventory methods, long-term obligations, taxes, dividend restrictions, and contingent liabilities.

Freight-In. Freight costs associated with purchasing inventory.

Freight-Out. Freight costs associated with the sale of inventory.

Funds Statement. Another name for the statement of changes in financial position.

Generally Accepted Accounting Principles (GAAP). Those accounting principles that provide the basis upon which external financial statements are prepared and upon which the independent accountants base their opinions regarding a company's financial statements. Since 1973, the Financial Accounting Standards Board has had the responsibility for establishing generally accepted accounting principles.

General Price-Level Changes. Changes in the aggregate prices of a wide variety of goods and services. These price changes are measured using a general price-level index such as the Consumer Price Index for all urban consumers (CPI-U).

Goodwill. An imprecise term referring to the excess of the purchase price over the recorded net assets acquired when one company purchases another company. Goodwill is shown as an asset only after it has been purchased from another company. No accounting recognition is given to internally generated goodwill.

Gross Profit. Net sales less cost of goods sold.

Historical Cost. Original cost; acquisition cost.

Income. The excess of revenues over expenses. Earnings or profit.

Income Statement. The basic financial statement that shows the change in owners' equity during an accounting period arising from the sale to customers of goods and services, less cost of goods sold and other expenses. The financial statement showing revenues, expenses, and net income.

Income Tax. An annual tax levied on the income of individuals and organizations by the federal and other governments.

Inflation. A rise in the general level of prices. A general decline in the purchasing power of a currency.

Intangible Asset. A non-current, non-physical asset. Examples are patents, copyrights, trademarks, and goodwill. All intangible assets must be amortized over a period not to exceed 40 years.

Inter-Period Tax Allocation. Income tax allocation between accounting periods brought about because of timing differences between when revenues and expenses are reported on the financial statements and when they are reported on the income tax return.

Investment Tax Credit (ITC). A direct reduction in a company's income tax liability granted by the federal government as an incentive to purchase equipment. The amount of the investment tax credit is calculated by multiplying a specified percentage (e.g., 10%) by the purchase price of the equipment.

Journal. The book of original entry where transactions are first recorded.

Last-In, First-Out (LIFO). The inventory costing method by which the cost of the ending inventory is determined from the cost of the oldest purchases, including beginning inventory, and cost of goods sold is determined from the cost of the most recent purchases.

Glossary

Ledger. The book containing a company's accounts.

Liability. A debt or obligation.

Line of Credit. An agreement with a bank whereby an organization has obtained previous authorization for short-term borrowings up to a specified amount.

Long-Lived Assets. Fixed assets purchased for use rather than for resale.

Lower of Cost or Market (LCM). A generally accepted accounting principle regarding inventory valuation that requires the inventory amount shown on the balance sheet to be the lower of (1) acquisition cost (however determined) or (2) current replacement cost (market).

Management Accounting. Provides internal users with quantitative information regarding an enterprise's resources, obligations, and financial performance.

Manufacturing Overhead. All manufacturing costs other than direct materials and direct labor.

Marketable Securities. Stocks and bonds that are readily marketable.

Minority Interest. The amount that represents the equity of minority shareholders in a subsidiary company that is shown on consolidated balance sheets either as a liability or as part of stockholders' equity.

Monetary Items. Assets and liabilities whose amounts are fixed in terms of number of dollars regardless of what happens to the general price level. Examples are cash, accounts receivable, accounts payable, and bonds payable.

Net Assets. Total assets minus total liabilities. Owners' Equity.

Net Current Assets. Current assets minus current liabilities. Working capital.

Net Income. The excess of revenues over expenses.

Net Loss. The excess of expenses over revenues.

Net Sales. Gross sales minus sales returns, allowances, and discounts.

Net Worth. Another name for owners' equity. In recent years, the use of this term has been discouraged.

Non-Current. Not due for a period greater than one year or an operating cycle, whichever is longer.

Operating Cycle. Normal time that it takes a company to recover its investment in inventory. That is, the average length of time between the investment in inventory and the subsequent collection of cash from the sale of that inventory.

Operating Expenses. Expenses incurred that pertain to the ordinary activities of the organization.

Owners' Equity. The excess of assets over liabilities. For a corporation, owners' equity is referred to as stockholders' equity.

Paid-in Capital. Represents the total amount paid by the shareholders for capital stock. Also called contributed capital.

Par Value. Face Value. Has no direct relationship to market value.

Past Service Cost. The present value of future amounts owed to employees at the time a pension plan is adopted for services performed prior to the plan's adoption.

Pension Plan. A plan whereby a company agrees to pay retirement benefits to its employees.

Periodic Inventory. A method of recording inventory that requires that a physical inventory be taken before financial statements can be prepared. A continuous record of inventory and cost of goods sold is not maintained.

Perpetual Inventory. A method of recording inventory whereby a continuous record of inventory and cost of goods sold is maintained. Physical inventories must still be taken, however, as a check on the accuracy of the perpetual inventory records.

Pooling of Interests Method. A method for accounting for business combinations whereby the assets and liabilities of the acquired companies are reported by the acquiring company at their previous book values. Fair market values are not used, and no goodwill is recorded.

Pre-emptive Right. The right of stockholders to maintain their proportionate ownership in a corporation by purchasing a proportionate share of any new stock that is issued.

Preferred Stock. Capital stock that is preferred as to dividends at a stated amount per share or as to the distribution of assets in the case of liquidation.

Glossary 173

Prepaid Expense. An expenditure made prior to the incurring of an expense. Prepaid expenses are shown as assets on the balance sheet.

Prior Period Adjustments. Items shown in the statement of retained earnings that represent material adjustments specifically identified with prior accounting periods.

Profit. Income.

Pro-Forma Financial Statements. Hypothetical, as if, or projected financial statements.

Purchase Method. A method of accounting for business combinations whereby the assets and liabilities of the acquired companies are reported by the acquiring company at their fair market value at the time the business combination occurred. Any excess of the total acquisition cost over the fair market value of the net assets acquired is reported as goodwill.

Raw Materials. Goods purchased for use in the manufacturing process.

Reserve. An overused accounting term with a variety of meanings whose use has been discouraged in recent years. Instead of "Reserve for Doubtful Accounts," a better phrase is "Allowance for Uncollectible Accounts"; instead of "Reserve for Depreciation," a better phrase is "Accumulated Depreciation."

Retained Earnings. Total net income over the life of a corporation minus all distributions of income in the form of dividends.

Revenue. The increase in owners' equity during an accounting period representing the sale of products or services. Revenue is measured by the inflow of net assets to an organization.

Salvage Value. The estimated future selling price of a fixed asset at the end of its useful life.

Short-Term. Due within one year or an operating cycle, whichever is longer.

Stock Dividend. A dividend payable in a company's own capital stock rather than in cash. Payment of a stock dividend has no effect on a company's assets or liabilities.

Stock Split. An increase in the number of common shares outstanding resulting from a corresponding decrease in the par or stated value per share of common stock.

Stockholders' Equity. The owners' equity of a corporation. Stockholders' equity is comprised of paid-in capital and retained earnings.

Straight-Line Depreciation. A depreciation method that results in equal periodic amounts of depreciation expense.

Subchapter S Corporation. A corporation with no more than 15 stockholders that elects to be taxed as if it were a partnership.

Sum-of-the-Years' Digits Depreciation. An accelerated depreciation method.

T-Account. An account shaped like the letter "T". Each T account has a title, a number, and a left side and right side.

Timing Differences. Differences in the timing of the reporting of certain revenues and expenses for tax purposes and for book purposes.

Treasury Stock. Shares of its own capital stock issued by a corporation and subsequently reacquired, usually by purchase. The cost of treasury stock is usually treated as a reduction in total stockholders' equity.

Trial Balance. A listing of a company's accounts and their balances prepared prior to the preparation of the company's financial statements in order to prove that the books are in balance; i.e., that the total of the left side account balances equals the total of the right side account balances.

Uncollectible Account. An account receivable that a company expects not to be able to collect.

Vested Benefits. Pension benefits to which employees are entitled upon retirement regardless of whether they continue to be employed by the company until they reach retirement age.

Weighted-Average Inventory Method. An inventory costing method by which both ending inventory and cost of goods sold are reported at the weighted average cost of inventory.

Working Capital. Current assets minus current liabilities. Also called net current assets and net working capital.

Work in Process. Partially completed inventory of a manufacturer.

Index

A

Accounting
    Accrual method, 26
    Concepts, 10
    Defined, 3
    Equation, 16
    Financial, definition of, 4
    Management, definition of, 4
    Nature and purpose of, 2
    Reports
        External, 4
        Income tax, 5
        Internal, 5
Accounting period, 11
Accounting principles, 7
Accounting Principles Board, 10
Accounts, 32-35
    T-account, 32
Accrual accounting, 26
American Accounting Association, 9
American Institute of CPAs, 8-10
Analysis of business transactions, 35-37
Annual reports, 91-114
Assets, 16
    Allocated cost, 20, 24
    Changes in, a manufacturing company 67
    Changes in, a trading company, 66
    Current, 52, 69
    Explained, 16, 19
    Management of changes in, 68
Auditor's Opinion, 111

B

Balance sheet, 15, 17
    Comparative, 46
    Form of, 44
    Illustrated, 17
    Preparation for financial analysis, 119-122
    Purpose of, 16
Bank reconciliation, 73-74
Book value per share, 133
Business entity, 11
Business events, 32
Business transactions, 32
    Analysis of, 35-37

C

Capital stock, 16
Cash and cash equivalent, 69-70

Classification, 75
On balance sheet, 74
Reconciliation, 73-74
Valuation, 75
Cash and cash flow, 69-90
Cash in bank, 70
Checks and deposits, 72-73
Collected balance, 71-72
Internally generated, 80
Cash flow statement, 79-81
Illustrated, 82
Cash management, 70
Cash receipts and disbursements, 76-78
Chart of accounts, 33
Collected balance, 71-72
Combined statement of income and retained earnings, 45-47
Compensating bank balances, 70
Conservatism, 12
Consignment, 19
Consistency between period, 12
Consolidated group of corporations, 93
Constant dollar accounting, 140
Consumer Price Index, 141, 158-159
Corporations, 5-7
Cost of goods sold, 23
Creditors, 17-20
Current assets, 52-69
Current cost accounting, 140
Current ratio, 69, 131

D

Debt ratios, 132
Depreciation, 24
Discretionary outgoes, 80, 83
Diversity in accounting, 12
Dividends
Date of declaration, 27
Date of payment, 28
Date of record, 27
Definition and requirements for, 27
Double-entry system, 32-33

E

Earnings per share, 93, 133
Earnings ratios, 132-143
Equity method, 83
Equity ratios, 132-134
Estimates, use of, 12
Executory contracts, 38
Expenses, 23
External financial statements, 4

F

Financial accounting, 4
Financial Accounting Foundation, 10
Financial Accounting Standards Board, 10
Financial reporting
Changing prices, 137-156
Objectives of, 138-139
Financial statements
Analysis of, 115-136
External
Limitations, 62-64
Objectives of, 112
Headings, 18
Financing and other, 80, 83
Fiscal year, 6, 19
Fraud and internal control, 87-88
Fundamental accounting concepts, 10
Funds, 110
Funds statement (*see* statement of changes in financial position)

G

Generally accepted accounting principles, 7
Going concern, 11
Gross margin, 23
Gross profit, 23

H

Historical cost accounting, 11, 112, 138

Index

I

Income from operations, 24
Income statement, 15
  Illustrated, 21
  Preparation for financial analysis, 117-119
  Purpose of, 21
Income tax reports, 5
Inflation
  Accounting for, 137-156
  Defined, 140
Interest, calculation of, 25
Interim reporting, 113
Internal control, 87-88
Internal financial reports, 5
Inventory turnover, 131

J

Journal, 36

L

Ledgers, 32
Liabilities, 16, 20
  Current, 52
  Definition of, 16
Line of credit, 71
Loan principal, 24

M

Management accounting, 4
Marketable securities, 75
Matching, 12
Materiality, 12, 113
Monetary assets and liabilities, 153-154

N

Net earnings, 22
Net income, 22, 25
Net income adjusted, 80, 81
Net profit, 22
Noncurrent accounts, 66
Nonworking capital accounts, 55

O

Objectivity, 11
Operating cycle, 69
Operating expenses, 23
Owners' equity, 16, 21

P

Pensions, 113
Price-earnings ratio, 134
Purchasing power gain or loss, 150-153

R

Ratio analysis, 126-134
Realization, 11
Receivable collection period, 131
Reconstruction of accounts, 57
Replacement cost disclosure, 140
Retained earnings, 27
Return on investment, 126-131
Revenue, 21-22, 26

S

Sales, gross and net, 23
Sandilands Committee, 140
Schedule of working capital changes, 54
Securities and Exchange Commission, 9
Statement of cash receipts and disbursements, 76-78
Statement of changes in financial position, 51-64
  Conversion to a cash flow statement, 122-126
  Form and content, 52-53

Illustrated, 60-61
    Preparation of, 53-57
Statement of financial position (*see*
    balance sheet)
Statement of income and retained
    earnings, 45
Statement of retained earnings, 26
    Illustrated, 28
Stockholders' equity, 16
Stockholders of record, 7
Supplementary inflation disclosures,
    140-142

T

Transactions, 32
    Analysis of, 35-37
Trial balance, 43

U

Uniformity vs. flexibility, 112

W

Work in process, 68
Working capital, 52